HISTORICAL ATLAS OF THE MUSLIM PEOPLES

T0391517

HISTORICAL ATLAS OF THE MUSLIM PEOPLES

Dr. R. ROOLVINK

Volume 28

Routledge
Taylor & Francis Group

LONDON AND NEW YORK

First published in paperback 2024

First published in 1957

This edition first published in 2008 by
Routledge
4 Park Square, Milton Park, Abingdon, Oxon OX14 4RN

and by Routledge
605 Third Avenue, New York, NY 10158

Routledge is an imprint of the Taylor & Francis Group, an informa business

© 1957, 2008, 2024 Djambatan N. V.

British Library Cataloguing in Publication Data
A catalogue record for this book is available from the British Library

Library of Congress Cataloging in Publication Data
A catalog record for this book has been requested

Publisher's Note
The publisher has gone to great lengths to ensure the quality
of this reprint but points out that some imperfections in the
original copies may be apparent.

ISBN 13: 978-0-415-42600-8 (Set)
ISBN 13: 978-1-03-258622-9 (pbk) (Volume 28)
ISBN 13: 978-0-415-44094-3 (hbk) (Volume 28)
ISBN 13: 978-1-315-88815-6 (ebk) (Volume 28)

DOI: 10.4324/9781315888156

HISTORICAL ATLAS

OF THE MUSLIM PEOPLES

HARVARD UNIVERSITY PRESS / CAMBRIDGE

1957

THIS ATLAS HAS BEEN COMPILED BY

DR. R. ROOLVINK

WITH THE COLLABORATION OF

DR. SALEH A. EL ALI

Professor of History at the College of Arts and Sciences, Baghdad

DR. HUSSAIN MONÉS

Professor of Islamic History at the University of Cairo

DR. MOHD. SALIM

Department of Islamic History, University of Karachi

WITH A FOREWORD BY

H. A. R. GIBB

PRODUCED BY DJAMBATAN · AMSTERDAM

Publishers & Cartographers

PRINTED IN THE NETHERLANDS

© DJAMBATAN N.V. 1957

FOREWORD

It is little more than a century since the foundations for the scientific study of Islamic history began to be laid by the recovery and publication of the major works of the Muslim historians and the classical Arabic geographers. The task, carried on at first by a small band of Western scholars and with the increasing cooperation in later years of scholars from all the Muslim lands, is still far from completed. But as the range of these studies widened, the need for a historical atlas of Islam became ever more apparent, and during the last half-century several projects were drawn up, and even begun. Unhappily, a number of factors combined to hamper, and finally check, these successive attempts to prepare a comprehensive historical atlas of the Muslim world. The vast extent of that world in time and space, its rapidly fluctuating political structures, the scarcity of available data for many areas in different centuries, all set a host of intractable problems. Political upheavals interrupted the collaboration needed for their solution, and the financial means proved inadequate.

It is high time, therefore, that the attempt should be made to break through the barriers of timidity and hesitation, to present boldly in cartographic form what is reliably known, to recognize frankly that much detail involved in any such presentation is provisional, and leave to future scholarship and enterprise the task of revision and supplementation. This Atlas is the result of that initiative. It is a happy augury that it should be the fruit of a collaboration between Western and Muslim scholars, and peculiarly appropriate that it should appear under an imprint which symbolizes the scientific association of South-Eastern Asia and the Netherlands, to whose scholars Islamic science in the field of geography especially owes an incalculable debt.

It is to be hoped that scholars who have made special studies in particular periods or areas of Islamic history will respond to the publishers' appeal to send in their observations and corrections. They will, at the same time, be the first to appreciate the extent to which this Atlas broadens their own knowledge and understanding of the sweep of Muslim history. Its wider service to the general public, and particularly in the teaching of history in universities and high schools, is too self-evident to require comment or commendation.

H. A. R. GIBB

CONTENTS

PREFACE

This atlas, with its limitations and imperfections, has the aim of being a sign of the times: in any case it is so that the compiler and the publishers have conceived it and intended it. The new awareness of Islam and the growing unity of the Muslim peoples are among the signs which today mark the beginning of a new historical era. At the same time the increasing cultural and political vigour of the Muslim peoples brings with it a greater responsibility, one which must be given a basis in a deeper consciousness of Muslim history and a more profound knowledge of the roots of Muslim civilisation. We hope – and believe – that this atlas can be of some help in providing such a basis.

Not only the Muslim peoples, but those of the entire world are in the first stages of a new confrontation of nations and cultures. In that confrontation the encounter with Islam as a religious and political force is just as engaging and instructive as it is unavoidable. It is our hope that also for non-Muslims who do not seek to avoid that confrontation, this atlas will prove a useful tool.

Through the ages various attempts have been made at delineating the geography and history of the Muslim peoples cartographically. In earlier times the Arabs themselves – such scholars as Ibn Hawqal, Muqaddasi, Ibn Khurdadhbih, Mas'udi, Ibn Rustah and Idrisi, for example – included many maps in their works. Though those maps are of great importance historically, the greater part of them depict only the situation in the fourth and fifth centuries H. (the tenth and eleventh centuries A.D.), and even that only partially, often without any indication of political boundaries or territorial changes. The limitations in the chartmakers' geographical knowledge and cartographic techniques

combined to produce maps which, judged by our modern standards, are rather less than reliable.

The Arabs also wrote a number of travel accounts containing a wealth of geographical data, but the authors of the accounts tended to limit themselves to places they had visited personally. Moreover the travel accounts – and the geographical works – are very chary of data regarding India, the Indonesian Archipelago and China, though there are several well-known exceptions, as for instance, in a later period, Ibn Battutah (mid-fourteenth century A.D.). The same applies to the geographical compendia. Practically all Arabic historical writing placed great emphasis on political situations and events. The writers described towns and countries and strategically important routes, they gave the dates of battles and conquests, but only rarely did they devote adequate attention to political boundaries, and as a rule the extraordinary and spectacular alone were deemed worthy of mention.

In recent times as well various attempts at charting the world of Islam have been made. The most comprehensive project of this sort was undoubtedly that of G. Le Strange, embodied in his three studies *Palestine Under the Moslems* (London, 1890), *Baghdad During the Abbasid Caliphate* (Oxford, 1900) and *The Lands of the Eastern Caliphate* (Cambridge, 1905). The last work is especially important, for, alongside a great deal of other valuable material, it provides maps of practically every province in the caliphate. However, Le Strange's descriptions pertain primarily to the situation in the tenth century A.D., the period of the greatest Arab geographers. Moreover, his emphasis is much more a geographical than an historical one. Other attempts have been the work of historians, who have tended to take a limited area as their field of research, so that the resultant studies are specialised in scope. The titles of the most important of these studies can be found listed in the bibliographies and reading lists provided in most standard histories of Islam.

The works which the general reader will find the most comprehensive survey of Islamic history are undoubtedly Carl Brockelmann's *Geschichte der islamischen Völker und Staaten* (Munich/Berlin, 1939) – which is also available in English translation under the title *History of the Islamic Peoples* (London, 1949) – and Philip K. Hitti's *History of the Arabs from the Earliest Times to the Present* (New York, fifth revised edition, 1951). However, in these two works Islam in India and Indonesia is left almost completely out of the picture.

In our times a person interested in the present and past of the Muslim world can hardly do without an atlas presenting the over-all historical and geographical picture of the whole Islamic world, with indications of places and boundaries, but at the same time also of the many changes that have taken place in relations within that world.

Therefore we feel that the *Historical Atlas of the Muslim Peoples* may well meet a real need. The atlas covers a period from the beginnings of Islam to our day, and includes all the territories to which Islam spread, from Spain to China. Delineating the various chief political centres, the shifts in power, the rise and fall of dynasties, we have attempted to give expression to the dynamics of Islamic history.

The atlas is, of course, not perfect, as we are all too well aware. We should have liked to present some maps in larger format, and some areas in fuller detail than proved possible within the compass of forty pages. We should have preferred to devote more consideration to various aspects of Islamic history – cultural developments, for example. And there are no doubt a number of points hardly touched on, or not at all, which should have been given ample treatment. We hope, however, that we will be able

to continue working on the atlas, correcting it, supplementing it and expanding it wherever it proves necessary. In this connection we should like to appeal to the kindness and knowledge of the users of the book, who, we hope, will not refrain from providing us with their constructive criticisms.

One of the many difficulties facing the cartographer of the history of Islam should perhaps be mentioned more specifically. That is the problem of boundaries. In writing on the subject one can often be content with such phrases as 'its power extended from A in the west to somewhere around B in the east, and from Y in the north to the neighbourhood of Z in the south.' Precise indications of boundaries are rare in the literature on Islam. In drawing a map, however, one is forced to indicate the borders between various territories as precisely as possible, and this has the disadvantage that as a result what was in most cases a fluctuating situation is stabilised and the border-territory character of the boundary is lost. In actuality the situation in the past was often that one travelled from one state to another via a sort of no man's land, hence most boundaries should be considered as approximate, and certainly should not be given the significance attached to a boundary in the world of today.

In a publication such as this one, not designed exclusively for specialists and scholars, we shall refrain from providing an exhaustive list of works consulted, limiting ourselves to the following acknowledgements. In our deliberations over what should be considered for inclusion in this atlas we have taken as a basis the works by Hitti and Brockelmann already referred to, and for India R. C. Majumdar, H. C. Raychaudhuri and Kalikinkar Datta's *An Advanced History of India* (London, second edition, 1950). Alongside these volumes a great deal of use was of course made of the *Encyclopaedia of Islam* (Leiden, first edition, four volumes and five supplements, 1913-1938), and also of such works as Edward G. Browne's *A Literary History of Persia*, four volumes (Cambridge, new printing, four volumes, 1951-1953) and other specialised studies published in book form or as papers in journals. For the map of the Indian Ocean special reference should be made to J. L. Moens' Dutch-language article *Çrīvijaya, Yāva en Kaṭāha* in Tijdschrift voor Indische Taal-, Land- en Volkenkunde (Jakarta), LXXVII (1937), pp. 317-487: a major portion of this study was published in a translation by R. J. de Touché in the Journal of the Malayan Branch of the Royal Asiatic Society (Singapore), XVII (1939-1940), Part Two, pp. 1-99.

We should in conclusion like to express our sincere thanks to the collaborators of this atlas. The broad knowledge, the interest and the critical sense of these scholars have been of tremendous importance for us. Many of their suggestions have been incorporated in this first edition, and our material has been supplemented by data which we should not have obtained without their co-operation.

Dr. Saleh A. El Ali of Baghdad revised the maps concerning the Middle East, and the data in the map on page two were contributed by him. Dr. Hussain Monés of Cairo devoted special attention to North Africa and Spain, and provided us with important data on these regions, as well as the map of Egypt in the Early Middle Ages. Dr. Mohd. Salim of Karachi supplied information on the Indian sub-continent. Without the collaboration of these eminent scholars the atlas would not have become what it is now.

Special thanks are also due to the many craftsmen, geographers, designers, lithographers and others at Djambatan who worked with such great devotion, and to Mr. B. J. Aalbers and Mr. F. W. Michels for their artistic help.

With this we present our work to its users. We hope that they may be numerous: the history of the Muslim peoples deserves to be studied, and known, by many.

THE PUBLISHERS   THE COMPILER

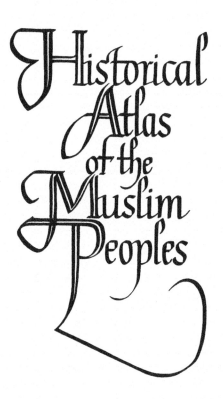

Historical Atlas of the Muslim Peoples

Map 1 (top): WESTERN ASIA from the FALL of ASSYRIA to the RISE of the PERSIAN ACHAEMENID EMPIRE 612–525 BC

Thracia
BLACK SEA
Byzantium • Sinope
Athénae •
Sparta • Sardes
• Miletus
546
Cappadocia
Crete
Cilicia
Tarsus •
Karkhemis •
Harran • Nineveh
539 550
Cyprus
Hamath •
Tyrus • Damascus •
Meggido •
Jeruzalem •
Gaza • Pelusium •
• Maan
Sais •
Memphis •
525
MEDITERRANEAN SEA
Libya
Babylon •
Opis •
Susa •
Ecbatana •
Rhagae •
Hyrcania
Parthia
Sagartia
Persepolis •
Tarva •
Harmozia •
Persis
Arrachosia
Khorasmia
Sogdia
Bactra •
Bactria
INDIA
Indus
CASPIAN SEA
Oxus
Euphrates
Tigris
PERSIAN GULF
Median Desert
Arabian Desert
Nile
Libyan Desert
Thebae •
Napata • KINGDOM
NUBIAN
ARABIA
RED SEA
Omana
ARABIAN SEA
Main
Marib
(Saba)
Hadhramaut

Legend (top map):
- Median Empire
- Chaldean Empire
- Egyptian (Saitian) Kingdom
- Lydian Kingdom
- Greece and Greek Colonies
- Territory of the Minaeo-Sabaeans
- Dates indicate Year of Persian Conquest

Map 2 (bottom): WESTERN ASIA in the 1st Century AD

BLACK SEA
Byzantium • Sinope
Ancyra • Trapezus •
Athénae •
Sardes •
Armenia
Caesarea •
Crete
Harran •
Antiochia •
Hatra •
Dura •
Arbela •
Media
Antiochia Margiana
Cyprus
Tyrus •
Palmyra •
Damascus •
Seleucia •
Rhagae •
Ecbatana •
Hecatompylus
Alexandria Arion
Alexandria •
Gaza •
Pelusium •
Jerusalem •
Bosra •
Petra •
Arsinoe •
Ayla •
Susa •
Persepolis •
MEDITERRANEAN SEA
EGYPT
Memphis •
Libyan Desert
Al-Qusayr •
Nubian Desert
Nile
Apologus (Al-Ubulla) •
Gerrha •
Harmozia •
Gedrosia
Suhar •
Omana
ARABIAN SEA
Al-Hijr •
Al-Ula •
Al-Hawra (Leuke Kome) •
Iathrippa •
Macoraba •
ARABIA
RED SEA
KINGDOM OF AKSUM
Aksum •
Sana •
Moza •
Zafar •
Dhufar
Aden •
Marib •
Hadhramaut
CASPIAN SEA
Oxus
Araxes
Euphrates
Tigris
PERSIAN GULF
Indus
INDIA

Legend (bottom map):
- Roman Empire
- Parthian Empire
- Nabataeans
- Palmyra
- Himyarites
- Sabaeans
- Trade Routes

0   100   500 Miles

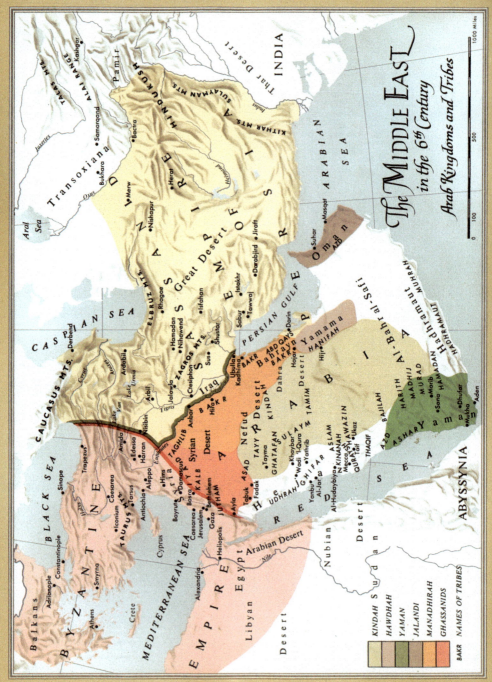

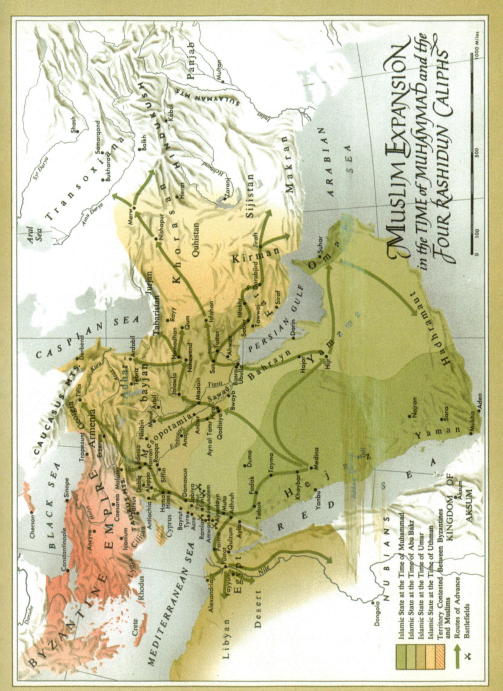

MUSLIM EXPANSION
in the TIME of MUHAMMAD and the
FOUR RASHIDUN CALIPHS

0   100   500   1000 Miles

Islamic State at the Time of Muhammad
Islamic State at the Time of Abu Bakr
Islamic State at the Time of Umar
Islamic State at the Time of Uthman
Territory Contested Between Byzantines
and Muslims
Routes of Advance
Battlefields

Aral
Sea
Syr Darya
Transoxi:
Bukhara
Samarqand
Shash
Amu Darya
HINDU KUSH
Balkh
Kabul
SULAYMAN MTS
Multan
Indus
Panjab
Herat
Helmand
Merv
Nishapur
Khorasan
Quhistan
Sijistan
Zaranj
Makran
CASPIAN SEA
Darband
Ardabil
Tabaristan
Jurjan
Rayy
Hamadhan
Qum
Isfahan
Kirman
Jiraft
ARABIAN
SEA
Adhar
bayjan
Tiflis
Georgia
Armenia
Tabriz
Nihawend
Susa
Tustar
Ahwaz
Sabur
Istakhr
Tawwaj
Sirjan
Darabjird
Fars
Siraf
Darin
Oman
Suhar
CAUCASUS MTS
Trapizunt
Erzerum
Mosul
Arbil
Jalawla
Madain
Sawad
Anbar
Tigris
Bwayb
Ubulla
Basra
Qadisiya
Ayn al Tamr
Persian Gulf
Bahrayn
Hajar
Hijr
Yamama
Hadhramaut
Erzurum
Malatiya
Edessa
Harran
Raqqa
Nisibin
Mesopotamia
Euphrates
Hira
BLACK SEA
Cherson
Sinope
Constantinople
Ancyra
Iconium
BYZANTINE EMPIRE
Lydia
Rhodus
Crete
TAURUS MTS
Cilicia
Tarsus
Caesarea
Antiochia
Aleppo
Qinnasrin
Hama
Hims
Damascus
Siffin
Palmyra
Duma
Tayma
Medina
Fadak
Khaybar
Yanbu
Najran
Sana
Mukha
Aden
Yaman
Tyre
Beyrut
Acre
Ramla
Jerusalem
Amwas
Ajnadayn
Muta
Adhruh
Tabuk
Hejaz
RED SEA
Jidda
Z.
Z.
Farama
Fustat
Ayla
Qulzum
Fayyum
Alexandria
Egypt
Nile
Libyan
Desert
MEDITERRANEAN SEA
Cyprus
NUBIANS
Dongola
KINGDOM OF
AKSUM
Aksum

3

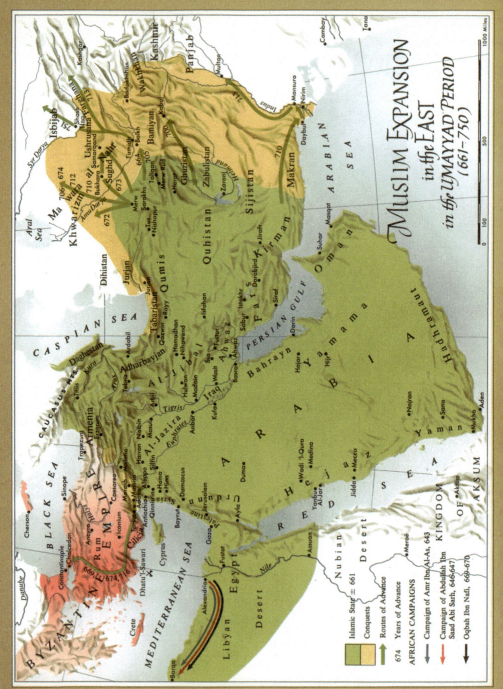

MUSLIM EXPANSION
in the EAST
in the UMAYYAD PERIOD
(661-750)

0   100   500   1000 Miles

Islamic State ± 661
Conquests
Routes of Advance
674   Years of Advance

AFRICAN CAMPAIGNS
Campaign of Amr Ibn Al-As, 643
Campaign of Abdullah Ibn
Saad Abi Sarh, 646-647
Oqbah Ibn Nafi, 669-670

4

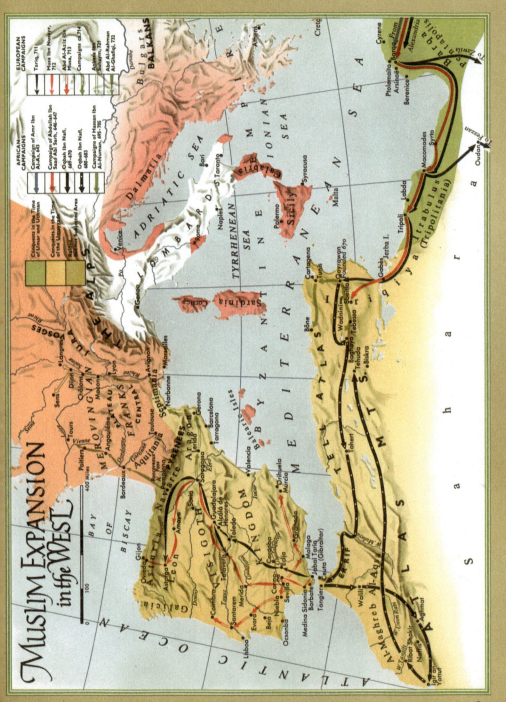

Muslim Expansion in the West

5

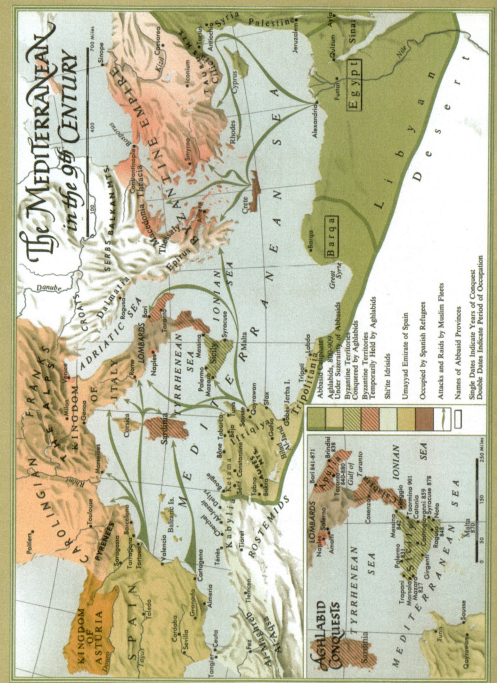

The Mediterranean in the 9th Century

700 Miles

Sinope

Kizil Caesarea
Iconium
TAURUS MTS. Cilicia
Smyrna
Rhodes Cyprus

BYZANTINE EMPIRE

Sirmium
Constantinople
Thracia
Macedonia
Thessaly
Epirus
Athens
Crete

SERBS
BALKAN MTS.

Danube

Sinai

Syria Palestine
Antioch
Jerusalem
Ayla
Qulzum

Egypt
Fustat

Nile

L i b y a n   D e s e r t

Barqa
Barqa

M E D I T E R R A N E A N   S E A

Alexandria

CROATS
Ragusa
Dalmata

ADRIATIC SEA
Bari
LOMBARDS
Taranto

IONIAN SEA

Great Syrte

Labda
Tripoli
Tripolitania

FRANKS
ALPS
KINGDOM OF ITALY
Rome
Naples
TYRRHENIAN SEA
Sicily
Palermo Messina
Mazara Syracuse
Malta

Milan
Vignier
Genoa

CAROLINGIAN

Rhône

Marseilles
Toulouse
Poitiers

PYRENEES
Barcelona
Saragossa
Tarragona
Tortosa
Valencia
Balearic Is.

Corsica

Sardinia

Bône Tabarca
Béja Souse
Tunis
ifriqiya
Sfax
Gabès Jerba I.
Qayrawan

Bilad
Al-Jarid

AURES
MTS.
Tobna
Bikra

Saint Constantine
Setif
Bougie
Kabylia
Al-Zazait

ROSTEMIDS

Al-Hazar
Tenès
Tiaret

Cherchel

Ketama
Delys

Balearic Is.

SPAIN
KINGDOM OF ASTURIA
Douro

Tagus

Toledo
Cordoba
Granada
Sevilla
Almeria
Cartagena

Tangier Ceuta
Fez

Tlemcen

Al-Maghreb
Al-Aqsa

Qayrawan
Tunis
Sousa

Abbasid
Caliphate
Aghlabids, 800-909
Under Suzerainty of Abbasids
Byzantine Territories
Conquered by Aghlabids
Byzantine Territories
Temporarily Held by Aghlabids
Shi'ite Idrisids
Umayyad Emirate of Spain
Occupied by Spanish Refugees
Attacks and Raids by Muslim Fleets
Names of Abbasid Provinces
Single Dates Indicate Years of Conquest
Double Dates Indicate Period of Occupation

AGHLABID CONQUESTS

LOMBARDS
Naples Salerno
Amalfi

TYRRHENIAN
SEA

APULIA
Bari 841-871
Brindisi
838
Taranto
840-880
Gulf of
Taranto

Reggio 901
Messina 842
Palermo 831
Marsala
Mazara 827
Trapani
Girgenti 827
SICILY
Catania
Comiso 859
Ragusa 848
Noto

Cosenza
CALABRIA

IONIAN
SEA

Taormina 901
Syracuse 878

Malta
870

Sardinia

Qayrawan
Souse

M E D I T E R R A N E A N   S E A

0   50   150   250 Miles

6

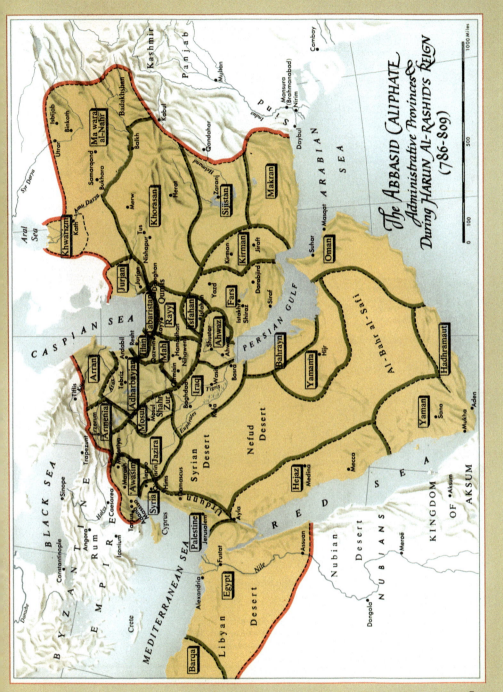

The ABBASID CALIPHATE
Administrative Provinces &
During HARUN AL-RASHID'S REIGN
(786-809)

0   100   500   1000 Miles

The ABBASID CALIPHATE
The Tahirids (822-873)
Situation Around 840

Abbasid Caliphate
- Under Direct Rule of Abbasids
- Tahirids (under Suzerainty of Abbasids)
- ⊙ Capitals

0 100   500   1000 Miles

BLACK SEA · Constantinople · Nicaea · Ancyra · Athens · Crete · MEDITERRANEAN SEA · Iconium · Tarsus · Edessa · Antiochia · Aleppo · Cyprus · Bayrut · Damascus · Jerusalem · Alexandria · Fustat · Egypt · Medina · Mecca · RED SEA · Hejaz · BYZANTINE EMPIRE · Georgia · Tiflis · Derbend · Armenia · Malatia · Tebriz · Adharbaijan · Al-Jazira · Mosul · Baghdad · Iraq · Syria · Khuzistan · Basra · Istakhr · Shiraz · Siraf · Fars · Bahrayn · PERSIAN GULF · CASPIAN SEA · Aral Sea · Syr Darya · Shash · Farghana · Bukhara · Samarqand · Amu Darya · Jurjan · Tabaristan · Rayy · Isfahan · Merw · Tus · Nishapur · Herat · Balkh · Khorasan · Kabul · Sijistan · Qandahar · Multan · Kelat · Kirman · Mukran · Daybul · Nirim · Mansura · Oman · Danube · Halys · Tigris · Euphrates · Nil

The ABBASID CALIPHATE
Ikhshidids and Hamdanids

- The Ikhshidids (935-969)
- The Hamdanids (Shi'ites); Mosul 929-991; Aleppo 944-1003
- Caliphate of Baghdad and Buwayhids
- The Fatimids
- The Qarmatians
- The Zaydits
- The Ziyarids
- Territories Conquered by Byzantines, 960-969, and later Regained by the Fatimids
- ⊙ Capitals
- → Fatimid Advances, 969
- → Byzantine Advances

0 100   500   1000 Miles

Sicily · Qayrawan · BYZANTINE EMPIRE · Athens · Kandia · Crete · Tripolis · MEDITERRANEAN SEA · Asia Minor · Rum · Iconium · Attalia · Cilicia · Adana · Tarsus · Marash · Antiochia · Cyprus · Hims · Syria · Damascus · Mardin · Mosul · Al-Jazira · Adharbayjan · Tebriz · Tabaristan · Hamadhan · Nihawend · Baghdad · Iraq · Kufa · Wasit · Basra · Bahrayn · Syrian Desert · Aleppo · Barqa · Alexandria · Ghaza · Jeruzalem · Ayla · Fustat · Egypt · Nil · Arabian Desert · Assuan · Hejaz · RED SEA · Medina · Yanbu · Mecca · Nubian Desert · Tigris · Euphrates

8

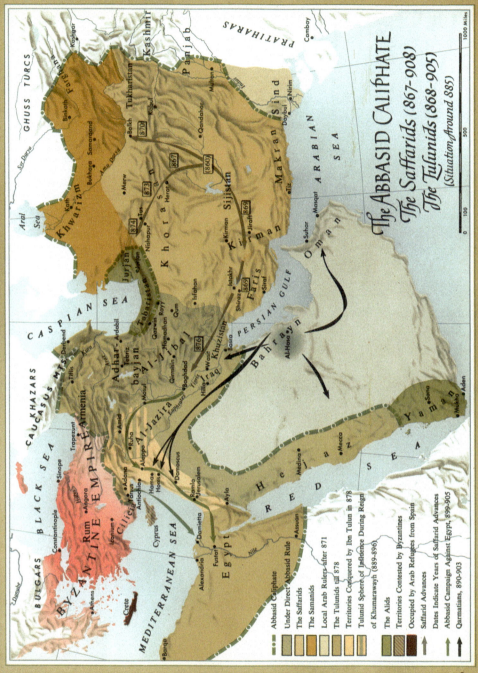

The ABBASID CALIPHATE
The Saffarids (867–908)
The Tulunids (868–905)
(Situation Around 885)

GHUSS TURCS

PRATIHARAS

Comboy•

Kashgar•

Kashmir

Sir Darya
Aral Sea

Farghana
Binkath•

Panijab
•Lahor
Tudut•

Multan•

KHAZARS

Khwarizm
Keth•
Kuba•

Tukharistan
•Samaqand
Bukhara•
Balkh 870
Amu Darya
•Kabul
•Qandahar

Makran Sind
•Daybul
Nirun•

BYZANTINE EMPIRE

CAUCASUS MTS.

Armenia

Ghuzistan

Khorasan
•Merw
Tus• 873
867
860
Nishapur•
Herat•
Kirman 869
Jiraft

Sijistan

Kirman

Daybul•

ARABIAN SEA

•Masqat

CASPIAN SEA

Jurjan 874
Tabaristan
876
Gurgan•

Ray•

Isfahan•
Qum•

Istakhr•
Shiraz•
Siraf•

Fars

Oman
•Suhar

BLACK SEA

Trapezunt•
Sinope•

Adhar-bayjan
•Ardabil
Derbend•
Tiflis•
Tabriz•
Kura
•Amid

Al-Jibal
Qazwin•
Hamadhan•
Qimisin•

Istakhr•

PERSIAN GULF

Bahrayn
Al-Hasan•

Constantinople•

Rum
Angora•
Iconium•

Cilicia
Tarsus•
Adana•
Antiochia•
Aleppo•

Al-Jazira
Ruha•
Mosul•

Iraq
Baghdad•
Tikrit•
Hilla•
Wasit•
Basra•

Armenia

MEDITERRANEAN SEA

Cyprus

Damascus•
Ramla•
Homs•
Hamae•

Ayla•

Hedjaz

Medina•
Mecca•

RED SEA

Yaman
•Sana
•Muluho
Aden•

BULGARS

Athens•

Crete

Barqa•

Damietta•
Alexandria•
Fustat

Egypt
Assuan•

Nile

Abbasid Caliphate
Under Direct Abbasid Rule
The Saffarids
The Samanids
Local Arab Rulers after 871
The Tulunids till 878
Territories Conquered by Ibn Tulun in 878
Tulunid Sphere of Influence During Reign
    of Khumarawayh (889–896)
The Alids
Territories Contested by Byzantines
Occupied by Arab Refugees from Spain
Saffarid Advances
Dates Indicate Years of Saffarid Advances
Abbasid Campaign Against Egypt, 890–905
Qarmatians, 890–903

9

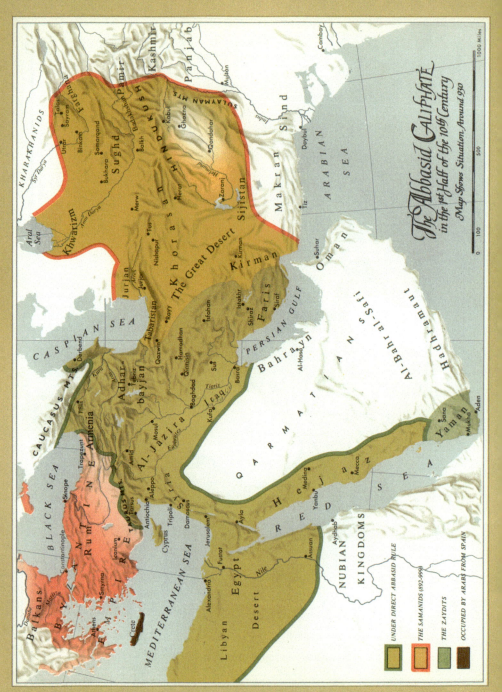

The Abbasid Caliphate
in the 1st Half of the 10th Century
Map Shows Situation, Around 930

KHARAKHANIDS
Sr Darya
Uiget
Isfijab
Soyran
Binkata
Farghana
Pamir
Samarqand
Bukhara
Khwārizm
Aral Sea
Amu Darya
Sughd
Balkh
HINDUKUSH
Kabul
Ghazna
Qandahar
SULAYMAN MTS
Badakhshan
Kashmir
Panjab
Qandohar
Sind
Indus
Merw
Tus
Nishapur
Abiv
Jurjan
Tabaristan
Herat
Zarani
Sijistan
Makran
Kirman
Kirman
ARABIAN SEA
Comboy
Mylan
Daybul
Tiz
CASPIAN SEA
Kuro
Derbend
Rayy
Qazvin
Hamadān
Qirmisin
Baghdad
Isfahan
Sus
Kufo
Basra
Shiraz
Faris
Isgakir
Siraf
PERSIAN GULF
Bahrayn
Suhar
Oman
Al-Hasaa
Board
Tigris
Euphrates
Iraq
Al-Jazira
Mosul
Hira
Hadhramaut
Al-Bahr-al-Saafi
QARMATIAN
CAUCASUS MTS
Kuro
ADHARbayjan
Tabriz
Trapezunt
Amid
Armenia
TAURUS MTS
Aleppo
Antiochia
Tripoli
Damascus
Jerusalem
Cyprus
Sana
Yaman
Aden
Mukha
RED SEA
Mecca
Medina
Yambu
Hedjaz
Ayla
Assuan
Aydhab
NUBIAN KINGDOMS
BLACK SEA
Constantinople
Sinope
Iconium
Smyrna
Athens
Crete
BYZANTINE EMPIRE
RUM
Balkans
Danube
Mytilene
MEDITERRANEAN SEA
Alexandria
Fustat
Egypt
Nile
Libyan Desert

0   100   500   1000 Miles

UNDER DIRECT ABBASID RULE
THE SAMANIDS (892-999)
THE ZAYDITS
OCCUPIED BY ARABS FROM SPAIN

10

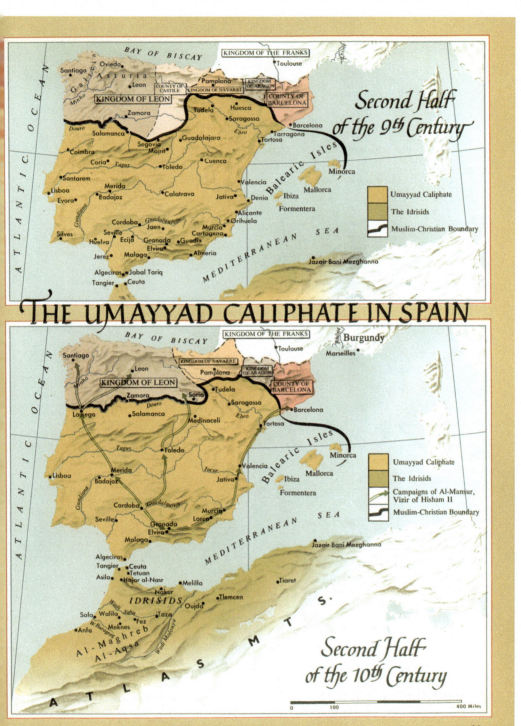

THE UMAYYAD CALIPHATE IN SPAIN

Second Half of the 9th Century

BAY OF BISCAY

KINGDOM OF THE FRANKS
Toulouse

ATLANTIC OCEAN

Santiago
Oviedo
Galicia
A s t u r i a
Leon
Minho

COUNTY OF CASTILE
Pamplona
KINGDOM OF ARAGON
KINGDOM OF LEON
Zamora
Tudela
Huesca
KINGDOM OF NAVARRE
Saragossa
COUNTY OF BARCELONA
Douro
Salamanca
Guadalajara
Barcelona
Ebro
Tarragona
Segovia
Majrit
Tortosa
Coimbra
Cuenca
Coria
Tagus
Toledo
Santarem
Merida
Valencia
Balearic Isles
Minorca
Lisboa
Badajoz
Calatrava
Jativa
Denia
Mallorca
Evora
Alicante
Ibiza
Cordoba
Guadalquivir
Orihuela
Formentera
Jaen
Murcia
Seville
Granada
Cartagena
Huelva
Ecija
Elvira
Guadix
Jerez
Malaga
Almeria
MEDITERRANEAN SEA
Algeciras
Jabal Tariq
Tangier
Ceuta
Jazair Bani Mezghanna

Umayyad Caliphate
The Idrisids
Muslim-Christian Boundary

Second Half of the 10th Century

BAY OF BISCAY
KINGDOM OF THE FRANKS
Burgundy
Toulouse
Marseilles

ATLANTIC OCEAN

Santiago
Leon
Minho
KINGDOM OF NAVARRE
Pamplona
KINGDOM OF ARAGON
KINGDOM OF LEON
Zamora
Soria
Tudela
COUNTY OF BARCELONA
Lamego
Douro
Salamanca
Saragossa
Barcelona
Medinaceli
Ebro
Tortosa
Tagus
Toledo
Balearic Isles
Minorca
Lisboa
Merida
Jucar
Valencia
Badajoz
Jativa
Ibiza
Mallorca
Guadiana
Cordoba
Guadalquivir
Formentera
Seville
Murcia
Lorca
Granada
Elvira
Malaga
MEDITERRANEAN SEA
Jazair Bani Mezghanna
Algeciras
Tangier
Ceuta
Tetuan
Asila
Hajar al-Nasr
Melilla
Tiaret
Nakur
IDRISIDS
Tlemcen
Oujda
Sala
Walila
Subu
Taza
W. Baregreg
Meknes
Fez
Anfa
Wadi Molouya
Al-Maghreb
Al-Aqsa
A T L A S M T S.

Umayyad Caliphate
The Idrisids
Campaigns of Al-Mansur, Vizir of Hisham II
Muslim-Christian Boundary

0   100   400 Miles

11

The 'Party Kings'

BAY OF BISCAY

KINGDOM OF FRANCE

Santiago

Leon

Pamplona

PALLARS · Cerdania

KINGDOM OF LEON

KINGDOM OF NAVARRE

KINGDOM OF ARAGON

COUNTY OF BARCELONA

PORTUGAL

Zamora · *Douro*

Tudela

Barcelona

Corsica

Saragossa

Tortosa

KINGDOM

Tagus

KINGDOM

Toledo

Valencia

Balearic Isles

Mayorca

Minorca

Sardinia

Lisboa

(13)

OF · Merida *Guadian*

OF

(12)

Jativa · Denia · Ibiza

(15)

BADAJOZ

TOLEDO

REPUBLIC

(5)

Cordoba

(13)

Murcia

KINGDOM

Guadalquivir

CORDOBA

(6)

KINGDOM OF GRANADA

(7)

Lorca

KINGDOM OF DENIA

SEA

OF SEVILLE

Silves

(1)

(2)

Seville

(14)

(4)

GRANADA

(3)

Malaga

Almeria

Tangier · Ceuta

(4)

MEDITERRANEAN

(1)	Banu Mozain
(2)	The Bahris
(3)	Banu Birzel
(4)	Banu Hammud
(5)	Banu Jahwar
(6)	Banu Ziri
(7)	Banu Somadih
(8)	Banu Razin
(9)	Banu Qasim
(10)	Amirids of Valencia
(11)	Banu Hud
(12)	Banu Dhu 'l-Nun
(13)	Banu Al-Aftas
(14)	Banu Abbad
(15)	Amirids of Denia

SPAIN after the Fall of the UMAYYAD CALIPHATE

The Almoravids
a Berberdynasty (1061–1147)

BAY OF BISCAY

KINGDOM OF FRANCE

Santiago

Leon

Toulouse

Pamplona

KINGDOM OF NAVARRE

KINGDOM OF ARAGON

COUNTY OF BARCELONA

Zamora

Tudela

Saragossa

Barcelona

PORTUGAL

Douro

Ebro

Mondego

KINGDOM OF LEON

Tagus

Toledo

Balearic Isles

▨	Territory Under Almoravid Rule Around 1100
▨	Ruled by the Banu Hud (under Almoravid Suzerainty)
▣	Capital, with Year of Foundation
◉	Secondary Capital

Lisboa

Zallaca 1086

Badajoz ✕

Guadiana

Merida

Jucar

Valencia

Cordoba

Guadalquivir

Silves

◉ Seville

Murcia

Cartagena

Granada

MEDITERRANEAN SEA

Malaga

Almeria

Jazair Bani Mezghanna

Bougie

Tangier · Ceuta

Qayrawane

Ashir

Qalat Bani Hammad

Melilla

HAMMADIDS

ZIRIDS

Tlemcen

B E R B E R S

MTS

Sala

Fez

A T L A S

Marrakesh ▣

1062

0   100   400 Miles

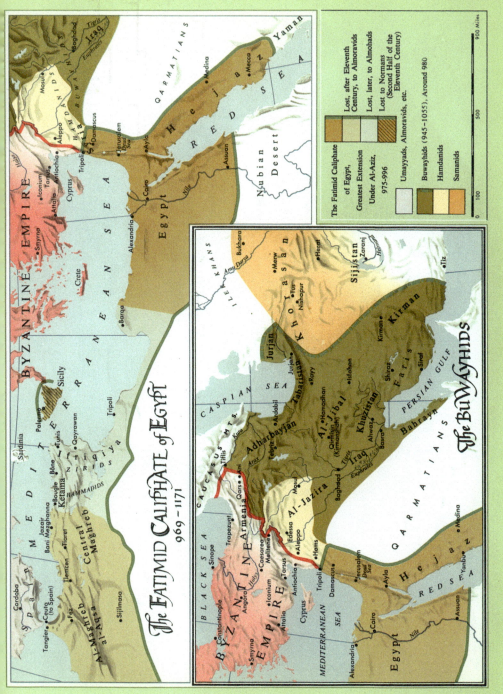

The Fatimid Caliphate of Egypt
969–1171

The Fatimid Caliphate of Egypt, Greatest Extension Under Al-Aziz, 975–996

- Lost, after Eleventh Century, to Almoravids
- Lost, later, to Almohads
- Lost to Normans (Second Half of the Eleventh Century)

- Umayyads, Almoravids, etc.
- Buwayhids (945–1055), Around 980
- Hamdanids
- Samanids

0 100 500 900 Miles

The Buwayhids

First map labels:

Baghdad, Tigris, Euphrates, Iraq, Mosul, HAMDANIDS, BUWAYHIDS, Aleppo, Damascus, Antioch, Tarsus, Iconium, Attalia, Smyrna, Cyprus, Tripoli, Jerusalem, Dead Sea, Ayla, Assuan, Cairo, Alexandria, Egypt, Nile, RED SEA, HEJAZ, Medina, Mecca, Yaman, QARMATIANS, Nubian Desert, MEDITERRANEAN SEA, Crete, Sicily, BYZANTINE EMPIRE

Second map labels:

Bukhara, Merw, Amu Darya, ILEK KHANS, KHANS, Herat, Zaranj, SIJISTAN, Tiz, Nishapur, Tus, Khorasan, Jurjan, Jurjan, Kirman, Kirman, Tabaristan, Rayy, Ardabil, Adharbayjan, Al-Jibal, Hamadan, Isfahan, Fars, Shiraz, Siraf, Qazvin (Kashan), Khuzistan, Ahwaz, Basra, Bahrayn, PERSIAN GULF, CASPIAN SEA, CAUCASUS MTS., Tiflis, Ani, Kutais, Armenia, Qars, Araz, Teflis, Al-Jazira, Mosul, Iraq, Tigris, Euphrates, Baghdad, QARMATIANS, Black Sea, Trapezunt, Sinope, Constantinople, Angora, Caesarea, Melitene, Edessa, Aleppo, Homs, Tarsus, Antioch, Iconium, Attalia, Smyrna, Cyprus, Tripoli, Damascus, Jerusalem, Dead Sea, Ayla, Yanbu, Medina, Hejaz, RED SEA, Egypt, Cairo, Alexandria, Nile, Assuan, BYZANTINE EMPIRE, MEDITERRANEAN SEA

Third map labels (western):

Cordoba, SPAIN, Tangier, Ceuta (to Spain), Fez, Sijilmasa, Al-Maghreb al-Aqsa, Tlemcen, Jazair, Bani Mezghanna, Tiaret, Central Maghreb, Bougie, HAMMADIDS, Bône, Qayrawan, Tunis, Ifriqiya, ZIRIDS, Tripoli, Sardinia, MEDITERRANEAN, Ketama

13

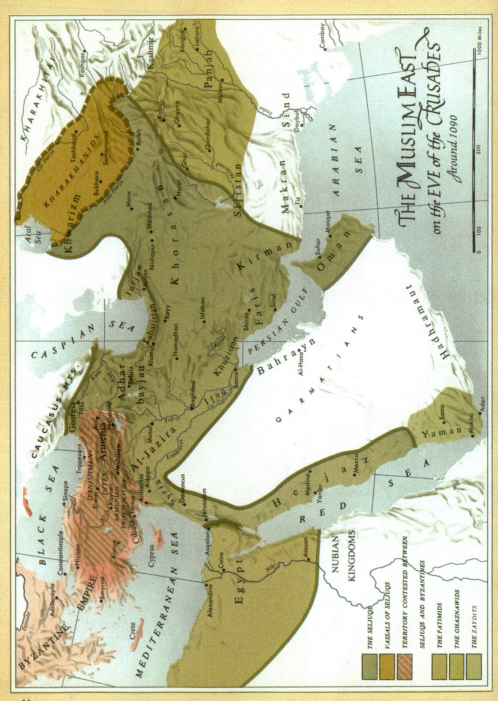

The MUSLIM EAST
on the EVE of the CRUSADES
Around 1090

0   100   500   1000 Miles

KHARAKHAN

Kashgar

Kashmir

Kongta

Lahore

Camboy

Panjab

Sr Darya   Toshkad

KHARAKHANIDS

Samarcand   Kabul   Ghazna   Gandahar

Bukhara   Balkh

Amu Darya   Marw   Ghur   Herat

S   i   n   d

Daybul

Multan

KHARIZM

Aral
Sea

Meshed

Nishapur

Juzjan   Gurgan   Rayy   Tabaristan

Alamut

CASPIAN SEA

Tabriz

Adhar-
bayjan

Kurv

Hamadhan   Istahan

Isfahan

Khuzistan

Karun

K   h   o   r   a   s   a   n

S   i   s   t   a   n

M   a   k   r   a   n

Tiz

Masqat

Suhar

O   m   a   n

A   R   A   B   I   A   N

S   E   A

K   i   r   m   a   n

F   a   r   s

Shiraz   Siraf

PERSIAN GULF

H   a   d   h   r   a   m   a   u   t

CAUCASUS MTS.

Georgia   Kuro

Tiflis

Ani   Dvin

DANISHMEN.

Trapezunt

Armenia   Molazgird

Sinope   Sivas   Kaysari

BLACK SEA   EL-DITEX   Malatya

ARMENIAN
PRINCIPALITIES

Tarsus   Cilicia

Constantinople   Nicaea   Konya

Smyrna

BYZANTINE
EMPIRE

Adrianople

Danube

Crete

MEDITERRANEAN SEA

Cyprus

Al-Jazira   Mosul

Baghdad   Tigris   Iraq   Euphrates

Aleppo   Antiochia

Syria

Damascus

Jerusalem

Aqalon

Cairo

E   g   y   p   t

Alexandria   Nile

Assuan

NUBIAN
KINGDOMS

Bosra

Al-Hasa'm

Bahrayn

Q   A   R   M   A   T   I   A   N   S

Mecca

Medina   Yanbu

H   e   j   a   z

R   E   D   S   E   A

Sana   Yaman   Mocha

Aden

Zaydit

14

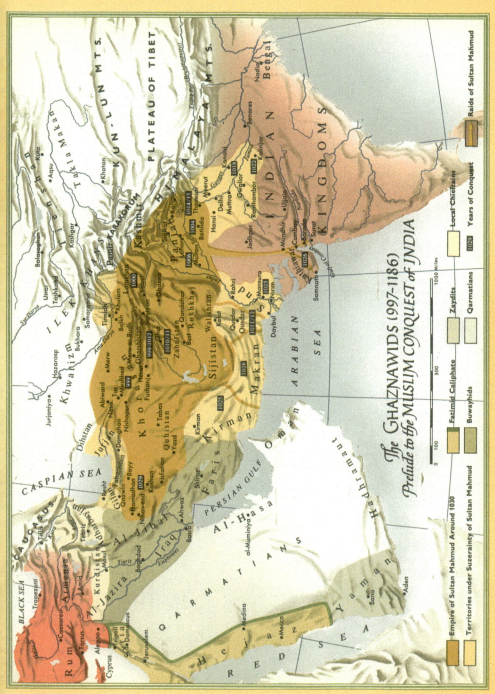

The GHAZNAWIDS (997–1186)
Prelude to the MUSLIM CONQUEST of INDIA

Empire of Sultan Mahmud Around 1030
Territories under Suzerainty of Sultan Mahmud
Fatimid Caliphate
Buwayhids
Zaydits
Qarmatians
Local Chieftains
1029 Years of Conquest
Raids of Sultan Mahmud

0   100   500   1000 Miles

15

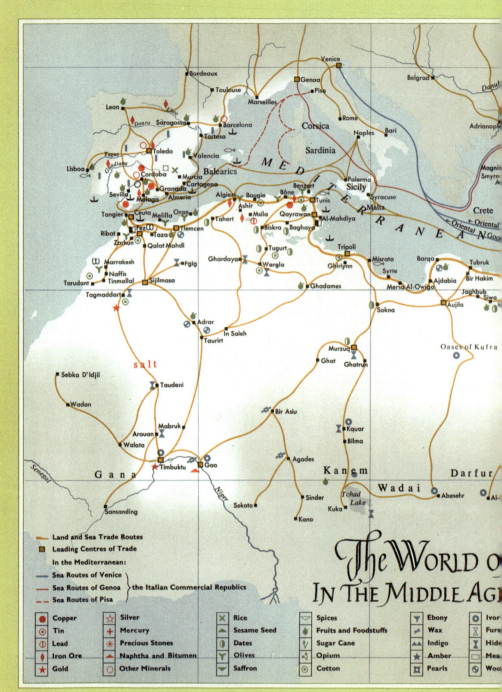

The World of
In the Middle Ag

Land and Sea Trade Routes

■ Leading Centres of Trade

In the Mediterranean:

— Sea Routes of Venice
— Sea Routes of Genoa   } the Italian Commercial Republics
-- Sea Routes of Pisa

● Copper	☆ Silver	✕ Rice	▽ Spices	▼ Ebony	◎ Ivor
◉ Tin	✚ Mercury	▲ Sesame Seed	✦ Fruits and Foodstuffs	⚡ Wax	✕ Furs
◍ Lead	✳ Precious Stones	◖ Dates	⋁ Sugar Cane	▲▲ Indigo	✕ Hide
◆ Iron Ore	▲ Naphtha and Bitumen	⋎ Olives	⊸ Opium	★ Amber	▢ Mea
★ Gold	○ Other Minerals	▽ Saffron	◉ Cotton	⊓ Pearls	◍ Woo

16

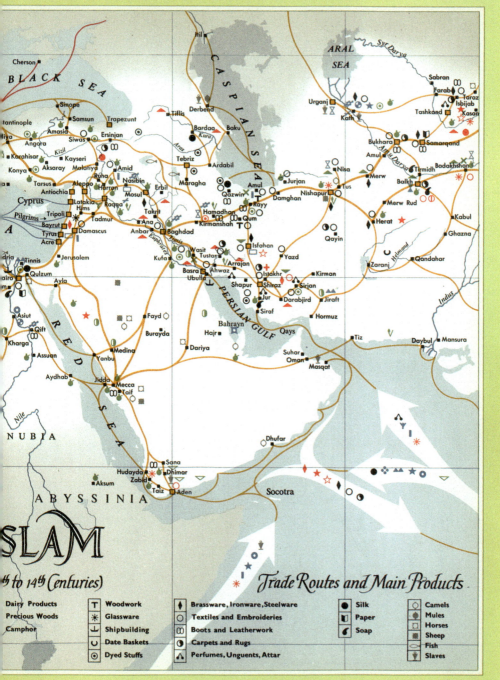

BLACK SEA
CASPIAN SEA
ARAL SEA
Syr Darya

Cherson
tantinople
liya
Angora
Karahisar
Konya
Aksaray
Tarsus
Antiochia
Cyprus
Pilgrims
A
Tripoli
Bayrut
Tyrus
Acre
dria
Tinnis
Jerusalem
airo
Qulzum
m
Ayla
Asiut
Qift
Kharga
Assuan
Aydhab
NUBIA
Nile

Sinope
Samsun
Trapezunt
Amasia
Siwas
Ersinjan
Kayseri
Malatiya
Amid
Ruha
Nasibin
Aleppo
Harran
Latakia
Hims
Tadmur
Ana
Damascus
Anbar
Baghdad
Kufa
Wasit
Tustar
Basra
Ahwaz
Ubulla
Shapur
Jur
Siraf
Fayd
Burayda
Dariya
Hajr
Bahrayn
Qays

hil
Tiflis
Derbend
Bardaa
Baku
Tebriz
Ardabil
Maragha
Amul
Qazwin
Rayy
Hamadhan
Kirmanshah
Isfahan
Arrajan
Yazd
Istakhr
Shiraz
Sirjan
Darabjird
Jiraft
Hormuz
Kirman
Kufa

Urganj
Kath
Nisa
Jurjan
Damghan
Nishapur
Tus
Merw
Amul
Bukhara
Samarqand
Sabran
Farab
Isbijab
Taraz
Tashkand
Kasan
Tirmidh
Bodakhshan
Balkh
Merw Rud
Herat
Kabul
Ghazna
Qayin
Zaranj
Qandahar
Indus

Takrit
Erbil
Mosul
Raqqa

PERSIAN GULF

RED SEA
Medina
Yanbu
Jidda
Mecca
Taif

Dhufar

Sana
Hudayda
Dhimar
Zabid
Aksum
Taiz
Aden
Socotra
ABYSSINIA

Suhar
Oman
Masqat
Tiz
Daybul
Mansura

Qum

SLAM

ᵗʰ to 14ᵗʰ Centuries)

Trade Routes and Main Products

	Dairy Products	T	Woodwork		Brassware, Ironware, Steelware		Silk		Camels
	Precious Woods		Glassware		Textiles and Embroideries		Paper		Mules
	Camphor		Shipbuilding		Boots and Leatherwork		Soap		Horses
			Date Baskets		Carpets and Rugs				Sheep
			Dyed Stuffs		Perfumes, Unguents, Attar				Fish
									Slaves

The Indian Ocean
From the 9th to the 14th Centuries

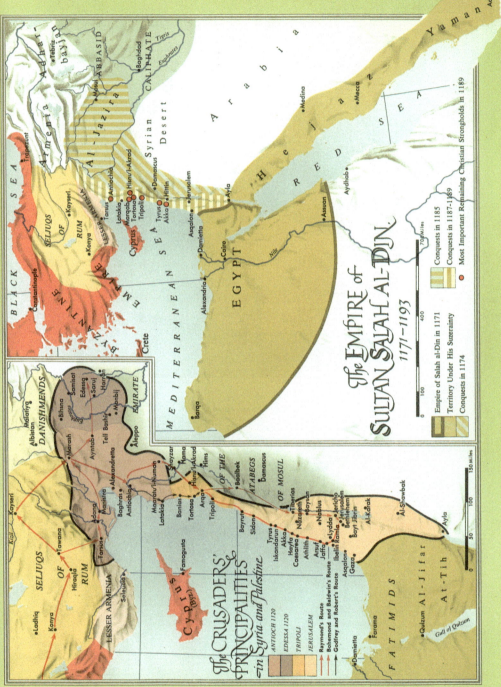

The Empire of
SULTAN SALAH AL-DIN.
1171–1193

Empire of Salah al-Din in 1171
Territory Under His Suzerainty
Conquests in 1174
Conquests in 1185
Conquests in 1187–1189
Most Important Remaining Christian Strongholds in 1189

BLACK SEA
Trapezunt
Armenia
Adhar-bayijan
Tabriz
ABBASID
Mosul
Baghdad
CALIPHATE
Al-Jazira
Tigris
Euphrates
SELJUQS OF RUM
Kayseri
Konya
BYZANTINE EMPIRE
Constantinople
Crete
Cyprus
Latakia
Tarsus
Antiochia
Marqab
Tortosa
Tripoli
Tyrus
Akka
Hisn al-Akrad
Hittin
Damascus
Jerusalem
Asqalon
Damietta
Cairo
Alexandria
MEDITERRANEAN SEA
Syrian Desert
Arabia
 Assuan
Nile
EGYPT
Barqa
RED SEA
Hejaz
Aydhab
Ayla
Medina
Mecca
Yaman
Aden

0   100   400   700 Miles

The CRUSADERS'
PRINCIPALITIES
in Syria and Palestine

ANTIOCH 1120
EDESSA 1120
TRIPOLI
JERUSALEM
Raymond's Route
Bohemond and Baldwin's Route
Godfrey and Robert's Route

SELJUQS OF RUM
Ladhiq
Konya
Hiraqla
Tawana
Kayseri
Kizil
Malatiya
Albistan
DANISHMENDS
Bihisna
Samisat
Edessa
Saruj
Harran
Menbij
EMIRATE
Maraş
Ayntab
Tell Bashir
Aleppo
OF THE
ATABEGS
OF MOSUL
Alexandretta
Baghras
Antiochia
Manistra
Adana
Tarsus
LESSER ARMENIA
Seleucia
Famagusta
Cyprus (Byz.)
Latakia
Maarra-in-Numan
Hisn al-Akrad
Arqa
Tortosa
Baniyas
Tripoli
Shayzar
Hama
Hims
Baalbek
Damascus
Tiberias
Nazareth
Baysan
Nablus
Jericho
Bethlehem
Bayt Jibrin
Lydda
Ramla
Jerusalem
Al-Karak
Al-Shawbak
Bayrut
Sidon
Tyrus
Iskandarun
Akka
Hayfa
Caesarea
Ahlihh
Arsuf
Jaffa
Asqalone
Gaza
Damietta
Farama
FATIMIDS
Al-Jifar
At-Tih
Quizum
Gulf of Quizum
Ayla

0   50   100   150 Miles

19

The Ghurid Empire of Afghanistan and Its Conquest of NORTHERN INDIA

0   100   400   700 Miles

	Ghurids Around 1190
	Conquests 1192–ca. 1205
	Empire of Khwarizmshahs
→	Their Attacks
	Indian Kingdoms

Tashkand
Khokand
Syr Darya
KHARA-KHITAI
Kashgar
Yarkand
Khotan
Bukhara
Samarqand
ALAI MTS.
Khorasan
Merw
Balkh
Badakhshan
HINDUKUSH
Tukharistan
KARAKORUM
Afghanistan
Herat
Ghur
Ghazna
Kabul
Peshawar
Indus
Kashmir
Qandahar
SULAYMAN MTS.
Jhelum
Chenab
Sialkot
Kangra
Panjab
Lahore
HIMALAYA MTS.
Kelat
Multan
Ravi
Sutlej
Batinda
Thanesar
Tsan Po (Brahmaputra)
Ucch
Tarain
Meerut
Hansi
Delhi
Budaon
Sijistan
Raor
Thar Desert
Mathura
Kanauj
Ganges
Benares
Bihar
Ajmer
Gwalior
Lakhnauri
(Gaur)
Makran
Brahmanabad
Ranthambor
Kalinjar
Brahmaputra
Daybul
Anhilwara
Ujjain
Nadia
Bengal
ARABIAN SEA
Kathiawar
Cambay
Narbada
VINDHYA RANGE
SATPURA RANGE
Orissa
Surat
Tapti
Bay of Bengal
Sind

The SELJUQS of ASIA MINOR

0   100   400 Miles

	Controlled by Seljuqs Around 1080
	Danishmend Dynasty Around 1100 Conquered by Seljuqs in 1180
	Conquered by Seljuqs Early Thirteenth Century
	Seljuqs of Iraq and Persia
	Eastern Border of Byzantium Around 1070
	Mamluk Sultanate of Egypt
	Kingdom of Lesser Armenia
→	First Crusade (1096–1099)

Maritza
Adrianople
BLACK SEA
Sinope
Samsun
Georgia
Trapezunt
BYZANTINE
Constantinople
SEA OF MARMORA
Nicomedia
Paphlagonia
EMPIRE OF TRAPEZUNT
Olti
Qars
Ani
Lake Sevan
Nicaea
Pontus
Amasia
Neocaesarea
Armenia
Abydos
Brussa
Angora
Erzerum
Malasjird
EGEAN SEA
Mysia
Dorylaeum
Kizil
Siwas
Lake Van
Van
Cotaeum
Lake Urmiya
Lydia
Galatia
Lake Tuz
Caesarea
Smyrna
Philadelphia
Antiochia
Cappadocia
Melitene
Amid
Ephesus
Apamea
Lycaonia
Albistan
Milete
Loodicea
Iconium
Heraclea
Marash
Caria
Isauria
TAURUS MTS.
Adana
Edessa
Mosul
Attalia
Tarsus
Mopsuestia
Manbij
Al-Jazira
Lycin
CILICIA
Seleucia
Antiochia
Aleppo
Rhodes
Laodicea
Hama
Tigris
Crete
Cyprus
Caesarea
Tortosa
Hims
SYRIA
Limassol
Tripoli
Euphrates

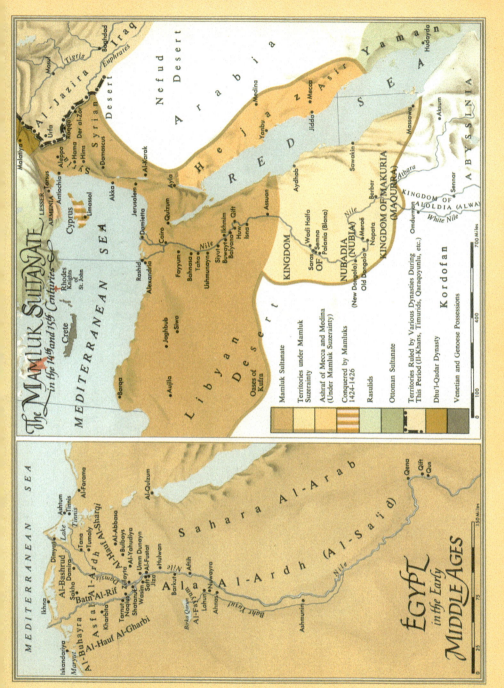

The **MAMLUK SULTANATE** in the 14th and 15th Centuries

Mosul
Tigris
Iraq
Baghdad
Euphrates
Al-Jazira
Urfa
Raqqa
Der al-Zor
Malatiya
LESSER ARMENIA
Tarsus
Antiochia
Aleppo
Hama
Hims
Damascus
Al-Karak
Ayla
Cyprus
Limassol
Akka
Jerusalem
Crete
Rhodes
Knights of St. John
MEDITERRANEAN SEA
Rashid
Damietta
Alexandria
Cairo
Quizum
Fayyum
Bahnasa
Toha
Ushmunayn
Siyut
Buwayt
Ikhmim
Balyana
How
Isna
Qift
Asuan
Jaghbub
Siwa
Aujla
Barqa
Kufra
Oases of Kufra
Libyan Desert
Nile

Nefud Desert
Arabia
Syrian Desert
Hejaz
Asir
Yaman
Medina
Mecca
Yanbu
Jidda
Hudayda
RED SEA
Aydhab
Sawakin
Mossaua
Aksum
ABYSSINIA
Wadi Halfa
Saras
Semna
Palania (Blano)
Meroë
Napata
Berber
Omdurman
Sennar
White Nile
Atbara
KINGDOM OF MAKURIA (MAQURRA)
NUBADIA (NUBIA)
(New Dongola)
Old Dongola
KINGDOM OF NUBIA
KINGDOM OF ALOLDIA (ALWA)
Kordofan

Legend:
- Mamluk Sultanate
- Territories under Mamluk Suzerainty
- Ashraf of Mecca and Medina (Under Mamluk Suzerainty)
- Conquered by Mamluks 1424-1426
- Rasulids
- Ottoman Sultanate
- Territories Ruled by Various Dynasties During This Period (Il-Khans, Timurids, Qaraqoyunlu, etc.)
- Dhu'l-Qadar Dynasty
- Venetian and Genoese Possessions

0 100 400 700 Miles

EGYPT in the Early **MIDDLE AGES**

MEDITERRANEAN SEA
Iskandariya
Ikhna
Maryut
Dimyats
Al-Bashrud
Ashtum
Tinnis
Al-Faroma
Al-Quizum
Lake
Tana
Soha
Demira
Tumoly
Al-Abbasa
Al-Buhayra
Tarnut
Kharbita
Al-Yahudiya
Naqiada
Sakha
Batn Al-Rif
Zufoyta
Wasim
Saff
Jiza
Hulwan
Al-Fustat
Umm Dunayn
Asfar Al-Ardh Al-Hauf Al-Sharqi
Al-Hauf Al-Gharbi
Shatanut
Barkun
Birka Qarun
Al-Fat
Lohun
Nuwayra
Ahnas
Ashmunin
Bahr Yusuf
Sahara Al-Arab
Ala Al-Ardh (Al-Sa'id)
Afih
Nile
Qena
Qift
Qus

0 25 75 150 Miles

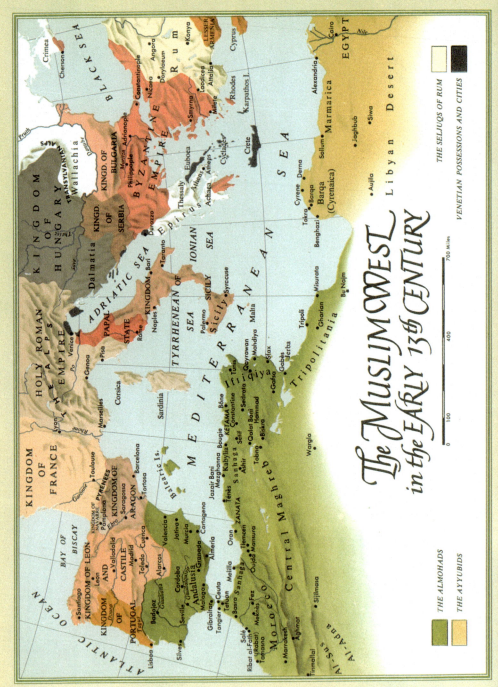

The Muslim West in the Early 13th Century

THE ALMOHADS

THE AYYUBIDS

THE SELJUQS OF RUM

VENETIAN POSSESSIONS AND CITIES

0   100   400   700 Miles

ATLANTIC OCEAN

BAY OF BISCAY

KINGDOM OF FRANCE

Santiago
Leon
Valladolid
Madrid
Toledo
Cordoba
Seville
Malaga
Granada
Almeria
Murcia
Jativa
Valencia
Cuenca
Alarcos
Guadiana
ANDALUSIA
CASTILE
KINGDOM OF LEON
AND
KINGDOM OF PORTUGAL
Lisboa
Silves
Badajoz
Tagus
Douro

KINGDOM OF NAVARRE
Pamplona
KINGDOM OF ARAGON
Saragossa
Barcelona
Tortosa
Ebro
PYRENEES
Toulouse
Garonne
Lyon
Rhône
Marseilles

Gibraltar
Tangier
Ceuta
Melilla
Oran
Tlemcen
 Oujda
Mansura
Fez
Meknès
Basra
Sale
Ribat al-Fath (Rabat)
Tamesna
Aghmat
Marrakesh
Tinmallal
Sijilmasa
Al-Adna
Al-Sus
MOROCCO
ZANATA
Sanhaga
KETAMA
Central Maghreb

Balearic Is.
Sardinia
Corsica
Genoa
Pisa
Venice
HOLY ROMAN EMPIRE
ALPS

Jazair Bani Mezghanna
Tenes
Bougie
Bône
Constantine
Sedrata
Qalaa Bani Hammad
Tobna
Biskra
Wargla
Kabylia
Sanhaga
Ashir
Serif
SAN HA GA

MEDITERRANEAN SEA

TYRRHENEAN SEA

KINGDOM OF SICILY
Naples
Rome
PAPAL STATE
Pisa
Bari
Taranto
IONIAN SEA
Palermo
Syracuse
Malta
SICILY
Tunis
Qayrawan
Sfax
Gabès
Jerba
Ghorian
Tripoli
Misurata
Bu Njim
Ifriqiya
Gafsa
Tripolitania

ADRIATIC SEA
Dalmatia
Durazzo
Epirus
Thessaly
Achaea
Athens
Aleppo
Euboa
Crete
Cyclades

KINGDOM OF HUNGARY
Save
Drava
TRANSYLVANIA
Wallachia
ALPS
Danube
Prath

Crimea
Cherson
BLACK SEA

KINGD. OF SERBIA
KINGD. OF BULGARIA
Adrianople
Philippople
Morava
BYZANTINE EMPIRE
Constantinople
Nicaea
Dorylaeum
Angora
Konya
R u m
LESSER ARMENIA
Cyprus

Smyrna
Miletus
Attalia
Laodicea
Rhodes
Karpathos I.

Cairo
EGYPT
Nile
Alexandria
Marmarica
Sollum
Siwa
Jaghbub
Aujila
Libyan Desert

Cyrene
Derna
Barqa (Cyrenaica)
Barca
Tokra
Benghazi

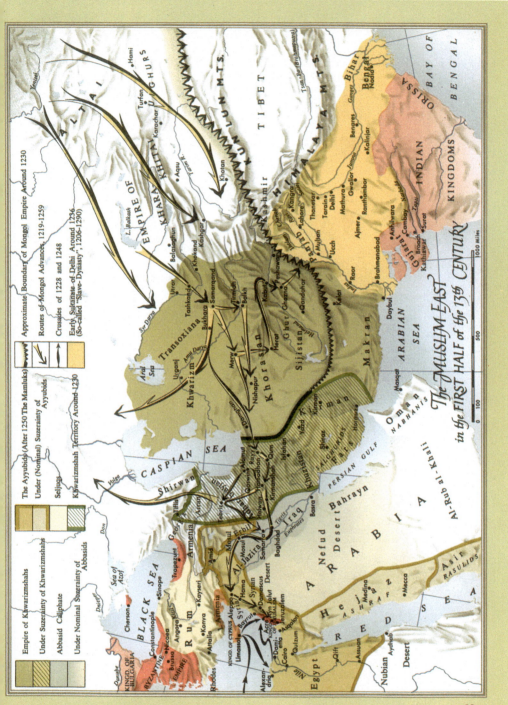

The MUSLIM EAST in the FIRST HALF of the 13th CENTURY

Legend (upper left):

The Ayyubids (After 1250 The Mamluks)

Under (Nominal) Suzerainty of Ayyubids

Seljuqs

Khwarizmshah Territory Around 1230

Empire of Khwarizmshahs

Under Suzerainty of Khwarizmshahs

Abbasid Caliphate

Under Nominal Suzerainty of Abbasids

Approximate Boundary of Mongol Empire Around 1230

Routes of Mongol Advance, 1219–1259

Crusades of 1228 and 1248

Early Sultanate of Delhi Around 1236 (So-called "Slave Dynasty", 1206–1290)

Map labels (selection):

ALTAI · UIGHURS · Hami · Yenisei · Turfan · Karachar · KUN LUN MTS. · TIBET · HIMALAYAS MTS. · Bihar · BAY OF BENGAL · ORISSA · INDIAN KINGDOMS · BENGAL · EMPIRE OF KHARA-KHITA · L. Balkash · Balasaghun · Aqsu · Khotan · Kashgar · Kashmir · Gujarat · Delhi · Mathura · Ajmer · Gwalior · Kangra · Benares · Kalinjar · Surat · Cambay · Broach · Kathiawar · Anhilwara · Surat · Transoxiana · Samarqand · Bukhara · Tirmidh · Balkh · Peshawar · Kabul · Ghazna · Gandahar · Kelat · Doybul · Makran · ARABIAN SEA · Muscat · OMAN · NABHANIS · Khiva · Urganj · Merv · Herat · Ghur · Sijistan · Kirman · Aral Sea · Amu Darya · Sir Darya · Tashkand · Khokand · Khorasan · Nishapur · Shiraz · Fars · Isfahan · Khuzistan · Basra · PERSIAN GULF · Bahrayn · Al-Rub al-Khali · CASPIAN SEA · Volga · Shirwan · Qazvin · Rayy · Qum · Kirmanshah · Hamadan · Baghdad · Mosul · Erbil · Samarra · Iraq · Tigris · Euphrates · A Nefud Desert · ARABIA · Hejaz · Medina · Mecca · ASIR · RASULIDS · RED SEA · Aydhab · Nubian Desert · Assuan · Qift · Egypt · Nile · Alexandria · Qulzum · Cairo · Damietta · KINGD. OF JERUSALEM · Jerusalem · Ayn Jalut · Damascus · Homs · Aleppo · Syrian Desert · Al-Jazira · Amid · Diyarbakr · Armenia · R u m · Konya · Kayseri · Sinope · Trebizond · BLACK SEA · Constantinople · Nicaea · BYZANTINE EMPIRE · Brussa · Rhodes · KINGD. OF CYPRUS · Limassol · Beyrut · Sea of Azof · Cherson · Don · KINGD. OF BULGARIA · Danube

Scale: 0 · 100 · 500 · 1000 Miles

23

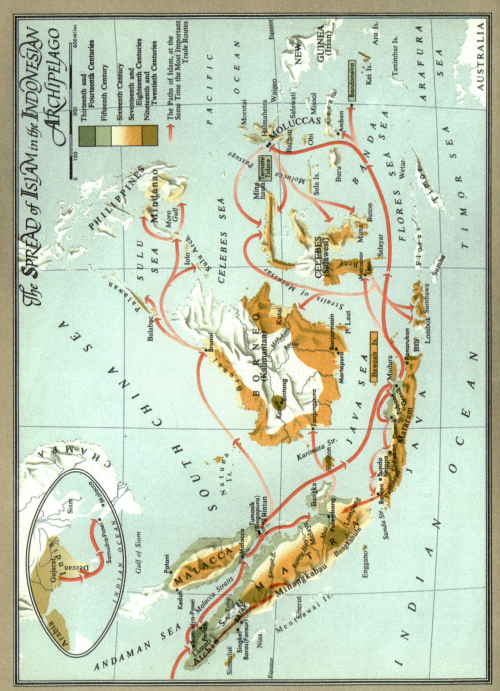

The Spread of Islam in the Indonesian Archipelago

Thirteenth and Fourteenth Centuries
Fifteenth Century
Sixteenth Century
Seventeenth and Eighteenth Centuries
Nineteenth and Twentieth Centuries
The Paths of Islam, at the Same Time the Most Important Trade Routes

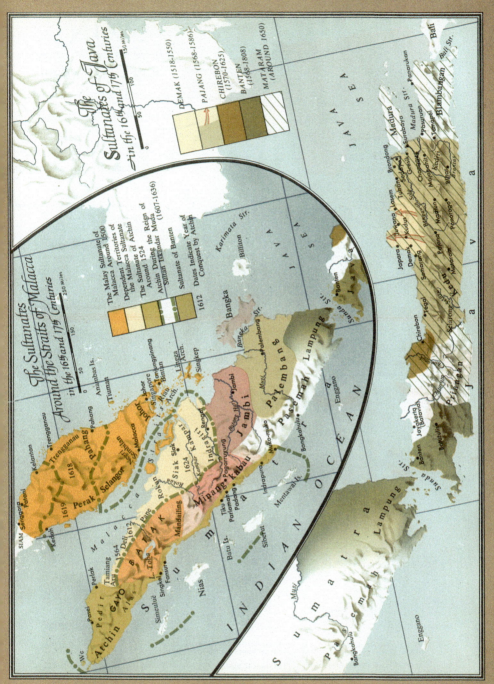

The
Sultanates of Java
in the 16ᵗʰ and 17ᵗʰ Centuries

DEMAK (1518-1550)
PAJANG (1568-1586)
CHIREBON (1570-1625)
BANTEN (1568-1808)
MATARAM (AROUND 1650)

0   50   100   150 Miles

The Sultanates
Around the Straits of Malacca
in the 16ᵗʰ and 17ᵗʰ Centuries

The Malay Sultanate of
Malacca Around 1500
Dependent Territories of
the Malacca Sultanate
The Sultanate of Atchin
Around the 1524 Reign of
Atchin During the
Sultan Tskandar Muda (1607-1636)
Sultanate of Banten
1612   Dates Indicate Year of
Conquest by Atchin

0   50   150   250 Miles

25

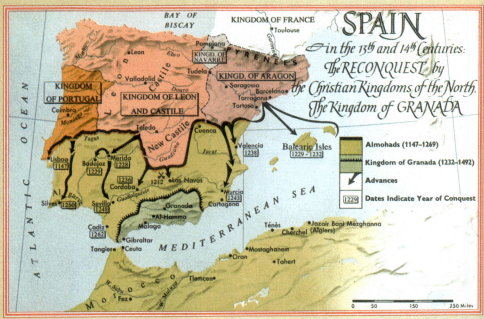

SPAIN *in the 13th and 14th Centuries:* *The RECONQUEST by the Christian Kingdoms of the North. The Kingdom of GRANADA*

BAY OF BISCAY

KINGDOM OF FRANCE
• Toulouse

Pamplona
KINGD. OF NAVARRE

• Leon
Valladolid •
Tudela
KINGD. OF ARAGON
• Saragossa
Barcelona •

KINGDOM OF PORTUGAL
Coimbra •
KINGDOM OF LEON AND CASTILE
Tarragona •
Tortosa •

ATLANTIC OCEAN

Toledo •
New Castile
Cuenca •
Valencia 1238

Lisboa 1147
Badajoz 1229
Merida 1228
1236
Cordoba
1212 • Las Navas
Murcia 1243
Balearic Isles 1229-1232

Silves 1250
Sevilla 1248
Granada •
Cartagena •

Cadiz 1262
• Al-Hamma

Malaga •
Tenès •
Cherchel •
Jazair Bani Mezghanna (Algiers) •

• Gibraltar
MEDITERRANEAN SEA

Tangier • Ceuta •
Mostaghanem •
Oran •
Tahert •

MOROCCO
Tlemcen •
Fez •

Almohads (1147-1269)
Kingdom of Granada (1232-1492)
Advances
1229 Dates Indicate Year of Conquest

0   50   150   250 Miles

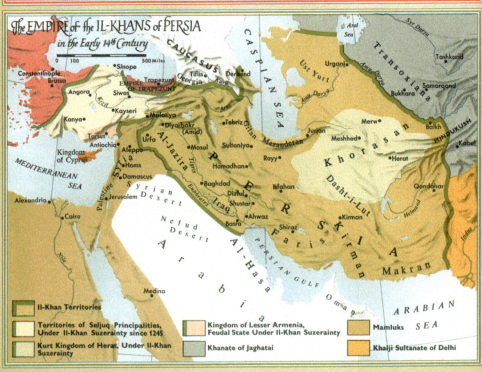

The EMPIRE of the IL-KHANS of PERSIA in the Early 14th Century

0   100   500 Miles

Constantinople
Brussa
• Sinope
CAUCASUS
CASPIAN SEA
Aral Sea
Syr Darya
Tashkand

Angora •
Tiflis •
Derbend •
Urganj •
Ust Yurt
Transoxiana
Samarqand

EMPIRE OF TRAPEZUNT
Trapezunt
Georgia
Kura
Amu Darya
Bukhara •

Konya •
Kayseri •
Malatiya •
Tebriz •
Gilan
Mazandaran
Merw •
Balkh •
HINDUKUSH

Tarsus •
Antiochia •
Diyarbakr (Amid) •
Sultaniya •
Jurjan •
Khorasan
Herat •
Kabul •

Kingdom of Cyprus
Urfa •
Aleppo •
Mosul •
Rayy •
Dasht-i-Lut
Qondahar •

MEDITERRANEAN SEA
• Homs
Damascus •
Hamadhan •
Isfahan •
KIRMAN
Makran
Helmand

Alexandria •
Jerusalem •
Baghdad •
Dizful •
Shustar •
Kirman •
Indus

Cairo •
Syrian Desert
Iraq
Ahwaz •
Faris
PERSIAN GULF
Oman

Nefud Desert
Basra •
Shiraz •

Nile
Al-Hasa

Medina •
Arabia
ARABIAN SEA

Il-Khan Territories
Territories of Seljuq Principalities, Under Il-Khan Suzerainty since 1245
Kingdom of Lesser Armenia, Feudal State Under Il-Khan Suzerainty
Mamluks
Kurt Kingdom of Herat, Under Il-Khan Suzerainty
Khanate of Jaghatai
Khalji Sultanate of Delhi

26

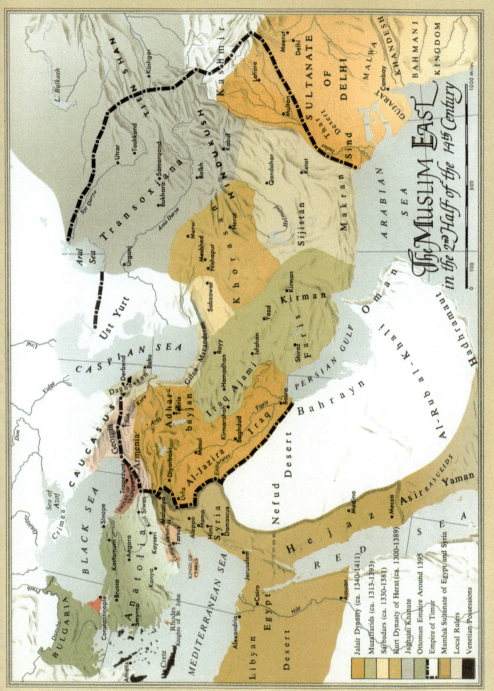

The Muslim East in the 2nd Half of the 14th Century

Map labels:

L. Balkash · Kashgar · TIEN SHAN · Kashmir · Meerut · Delhi · SULTANATE OF DELHI · MALWA · KHANDESH · BAHMANI KINGDOM

Utrar · Tashkend · Samarqand · Lahore · Thar Desert · Sind · GUJARAT · Comboy

Aral Sea · Syr Darya · Bukhara · Transoxiana · HINDUKUSH · Balkh · Kabul · Multan · Indus · Makran · ARABIAN SEA · 1000 Miles

Urganj · Amu Darya · Merw · Khorasan · Herat · Qandahar · Kelat · 500

Ust Yurt · Meshhed · Nishapur · Sijistan · Helmand · 100

Sabzewar · Royy · Gilan-Mazanderan · Hamadhan · Yazd · Kirman · 0

CASPIAN SEA · Baku · Derbend · Adharbayjan · Tebriz · Isfahan · Fars · Shiraz · Oman · Al-Rub'a-l-Khali · Haḍhramaut

Volga · Dagestan · Tiflis · Kura · Araxes · Iraq Ajami · Kirmanshah · PERSIAN GULF · Bahrayn

CAUCASUS · Georgia · Armenia · Mosul · Baghdad · Iraq · Tigris · Basra

Sea of Azof · Trebizond · Erzerum · Diyarbakr · Al-Jazira · Euphrates · Nefud Desert

Crimea · BLACK SEA · Sinope · Sivas · Malatiya · Urfa · RASSULIDS · Yaman

Don · Kastamuni · Kill Sivas · Aleppo · Hims · Hama · Syria · Mecca · Asir · Medina

Dnieper · Angora · Kayseri · Erzinjan · Jerusalem · Hejaz · RED SEA

Athens · Brussa · Konya · KINGDOM OF CYPRUS · Damascus · Cairo · Aswan

Constantinople · Smyrna · Rhodes · Knights of St. John · Jerusalem · Libyan Desert · Egypt · Nile

BULGARIA · Anatolia · Crete · MEDITERRANEAN SEA · Alexandria

Danube · Pruth

Legend:

Jalair Dynasty (ca. 1340-1411)
Muzaffarids (ca. 1313-1393)
Sarbadars (ca. 1330-1381)
Kurt Dynasty of Herat (ca. 1300-1389)
Jaghatai Khanate
Ottoman Empire Around 1395
Empire of Timur
Mamluk Sultanate of Egypt and Syria
Local Rulers
Venetian Possessions

27

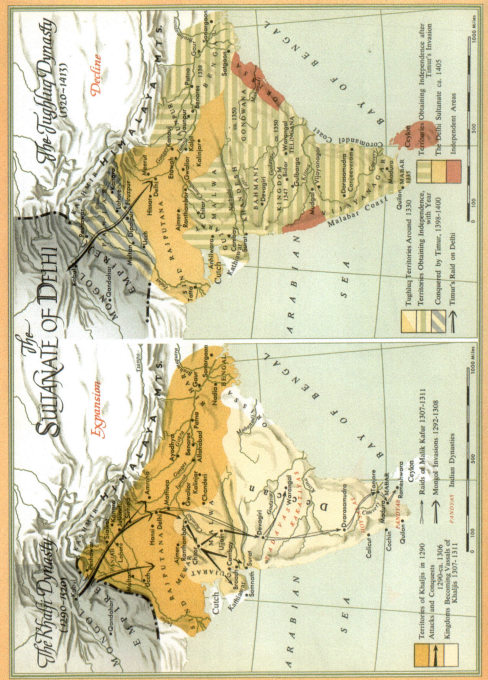

The SULTANATE OF DELHI

The Tughluq Dynasty (1320–1413)
Decline

HIMALAYA MTS.

KASHMIR

Kabul • Gandahar • MONGOL EMPIRE

Peshawar • Kangra • Lahore • Firozpur • Delhi • Meerut • Etawah • Kanouj • Gwalior • Kalpi • Benares • Jaunpur • Patna • Gaur • Sonargaon • BENGAL

Multan • Dipalpur • Hissar • Ranthambor • Kalinjar 1338

Uch • RAJPUTANA • Chitor • MALWA • ca.1350

Tatta • SIND • Ajmer • GONDWANA • ca.1350 • ORISSA • Mangalal

CUTCH • GUJARAT • Ahilwara • Cambay • Narbada • KHANDESH • Devagiri • Warangal • TELINGANA • Godaveri • BAHMANI KINGDOM 1347 • Bidar • Gulbarga • Dorasomudra • Vijayanagar • VIJAYANAGAR

Kathiawar • Surat • Bombay

A R A B I A N   S E A

Conjeeveram • Coromandel Coast

Quilon • Madura • MABAR 1335

Malabar Coast • Ceylon

B A Y   O F   B E N G A L

Legend (left):

Tughluq Territories Around 1330
Territories Obtaining Independence, with Year
Conquered by Timur, 1398–1400
Timur's Raid on Delhi

Territories Obtaining Independence after Timur's Invasion
The Delhi Sultanate ca. 1405
Independent Areas

0 100 500 1000 Miles

The Khalji Dynasty (1290–1320)
Expansion

HIMALAYA MTS.

KASHMIR

Kabul • Gandahar • MONGOL EMPIRE

Peshawar • PUNJAB • Sialkot • Lahore • Jullundur • Simur • Hansi • Delhi • Amroha • Mathura • Ayodhya • Benares • Patna • Gaur • Sonargaon • BENGAL

Multan • Uch • Ramhambor • Gwalior • Kalinjar • Chandeli • Allahabad • Nadia

SIND • RAJPUTANA • Ajmer • MEWAR • Chitor • MALWA • Ujjain • Kalinjar

Tatta • Cutch • GUJARAT • Cambay • Brooch • Devagiri • YADAVAS • Warangal • KAKATIYAS • Godaveri • HOYSALAS

Somnath • Kathiawar • Surat

A R A B I A N   S E A

Dvarasomudra • PANDYAS • Kaveri • Tanjore • Rameshwara • Ceylon

Calicut • Cochin • Quilon • Madura • MABAR

B A Y   O F   B E N G A L   Mahanadi

Legend (right):

Territories of Khaljis in 1290
Attacks and Conquests
Kingdoms Becoming Vassals of Khaljis 1307–1311

Raids of Malik Kafur 1307–1311
Mongol Invasions 1292–1308
PANDYAS Indian Dynasties

0 100 500 1000 Miles

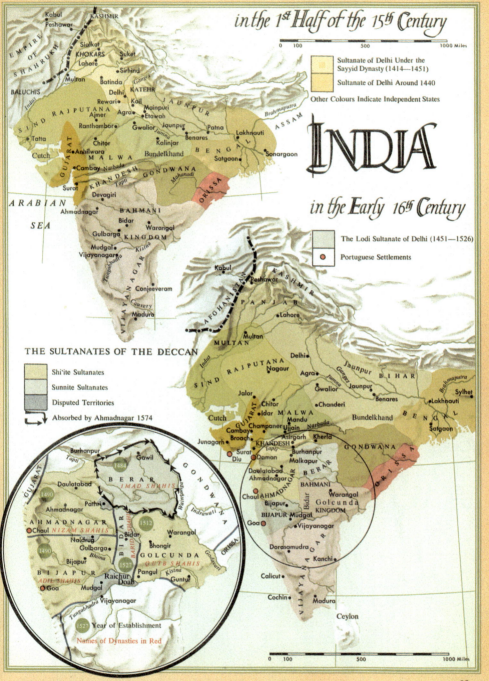

in the 1ˢᵗ Half of the 15ᵗʰ Century

0   100   500   1000 Miles

Sultanate of Delhi Under the
Sayyid Dynasty (1414—1451)

Sultanate of Delhi Around 1440

Other Colours Indicate Independent States

INDIA

in the Early 16ᵗʰ Century

The Lodi Sultanate of Delhi (1451—1526)

Portuguese Settlements

THE SULTANATES OF THE DECCAN

Shi'ite Sultanates

Sunnite Sultanates

Disputed Territories

Absorbed by Ahmadnagar 1574

EMPIRE OF SHAHRUKH

KASHMIR
Kabul
Peshawar
Sialkot
KHOKARS
Lahore
Suket
Sirhind
Multan
BALUCHIS
Batinda
KATEHR
Delhi
Rewari
Koil
RAJPUTANA
Ajmer
Agra
Mainpuri
JAUNPUR
Ranthambor
Etawah
Gwalior
Jaunpur
Patna
ASSAM
Tatta
Chitor
Kalinjar
Benares
Lakhnauti
Cutch
Anhilwara
Bundelkhand
BENGAL
MALWA
Satgaon
Sonargaon
Cambay
GONDWANA
KHANDESH
Surat
ORISSA
Devagiri
Ahmadnagar
BAHMANI
Bidar
Warangal
Gulbarga
KINGDOM
Mudgal
Vijayanagara
Conjeeveram
VIJAYANAGAR
Madura

ARABIAN SEA

SIND GUJARAT Narbada Tapti Mahanadi Kistna Tungabhadra Cauvery

Kabul
Peshawar
KASHMIR
AFGHANISTAN
PANJAB
Lahore
Multan
MULTAN
SIND
RAJPUTANA
Nagaur
Delhi
Jaunpur
BIHAR
Agra
Gwalior
Jaunpur
Benares
Lakhnauti
Jalor
Chanderi
Sylhet
Chitor
MALWA
Idar
Cutch
GUJARAT
Mandu
Champaner
Ujjain
Junagarh
Asirgarh
Kherla
GONDWANA
Cambay
Broach
KHANDESH
Surat
Burhanpur
Diu
Daman
Malkapur
BERAR
Daulatabad
BAHMANI
ORISSA
Chaul
AHMADNAGAR
Bidar
Warangal
Bijapur
Golcunda
BIJAPUR
Mudgal
KINGDOM
Goa
Vijayanagar
Dorasamudra
Kanchi
Calicut
VIJAYANAGAR
Cochin
Madura
Ceylon

Brahmaputra Ganges Jumna Narbada Tapti Kistna

THE SULTANATES OF THE DECCAN inset:

Burhanpur
Tapti
Gawil
1484
GONDWANA
Daulatabad
BERAR
IMAD SHAHIS
Pathri
1490
Ahmadnagar
Wainganga
AHMADNAGAR
Chaul
NIZAM SHAHIS
Naldrug
Bidar
1512
Warangal
Gulbarga
Bhina
BARIDAR SHAHIS
Bhongir
Indrawati
Bijapur
GOLCUNDA
1490
QUTB SHAHIS
ORISSA
BIJAPUR
Raichur
Pangul
Kistna
ADIL SHAHIS
1527
Doab
Guntur
Goa
Mudgal
Godavari
Tungabhadra Vijayanagar
1527 Year of Establishment
Names of Dynasties in Red

29

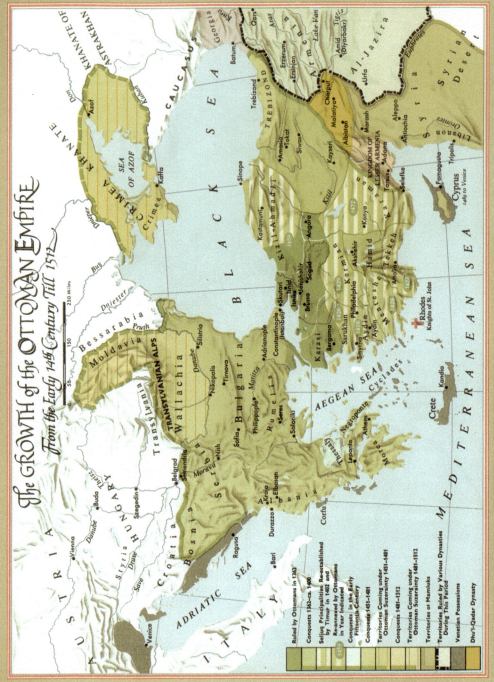

The GROWTH of the OTTOMAN EMPIRE
From the Early 14th Century Till 1512

KHANATE OF ASTRAKHAN

KHANATE

Don

Kuban

Azof

SEA OF AZOF

CRIMEA

Kaffa

Crimea

Dnieper

Bug

Dniester

250 Miles

50   150

Bessarabia

Moldavia

Pruth

Danube

TRANSYLVANIAN ALPS

Transylvania

Wallachia

Silistria

Nikopolis

Tirnovo

AUSTRIA

Styria   HUNGARY

Vienna

Danube

Buda

Szegedin

Drave

Save

Belgrad

Semendria

Nissh

Morava

Sofia

Bulgaria

Philippople

Maritza

Adrianople

Serres

Rumelia

Soloniki

Thessaly

Leponto

Moré a

Athens

Negroponte

Cyclades

AEGEAN SEA

Crete

Kandia

MEDITERRANEAN SEA

Serbia

Bosnia

Croatia

Ragusa

ADRIATIC SEA

Bari

Venice

ITALY

Durazzo

Corfu

Al-bania

Akroia

Elbasan

BLACK SEA

Sinope

Kastamuni

Angora

Kizil-Ahmadli

Amasia

Tokat

Sivas

Kizil

Kermian

Akshehir

Hamid

Tekke

Konya

Karasi

Bergama

Smyrna

Sarukhan

Aydin

Menteshe

Aïdin

Bursa

Germian

Skutari

Iznid

Ismid

Eskishehir

Constantinople (Istanbul)

Philadelphia

Karasi

Rhodes
Knights of St. John

CYPRUS
1489 to Venice

Famagusta

Tripolis

Selefka

Tarsus

Adana

KINGDOM OF LESSER ARMENIA

Antiochia

Aleppo

Orontes

Lebanon

SYRIA

Syrian Desert

Euphrates

Al-Jazira

Amid (Diyarbakr)

Urfa

Marash

Malatiya

Albistañ

Charput

ARMENIA

Erzinjan

Erzerum

Lake Van

Aras

Qars

Kara

Georgia

Batum

CAUCASUS

Trebizond

TREBIZOND

Tigris

Kayseri

Seguid

Kiz

30

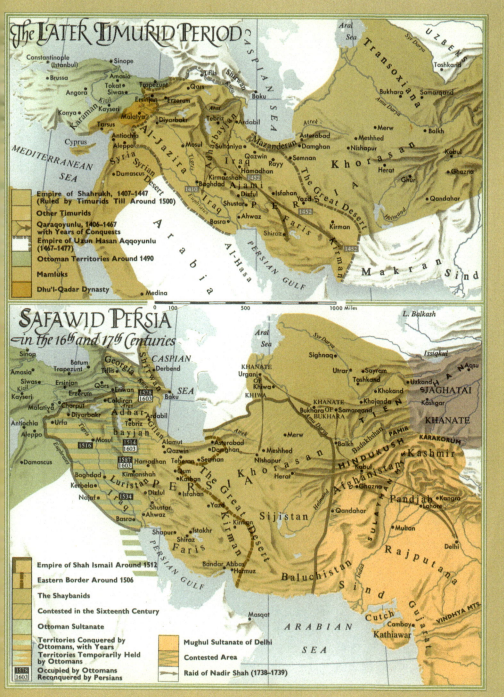

The LATER TIMURID PERIOD

MEDITERRANEAN SEA

Constantinople (Istanbul)
Brussa
Amasia
Angora
Sinope
Tokat
Siwas
Konya
Kayseri
Karaman
Tarsus
Antiochia
Aleppo
Cyprus
Trapezunt
Erzinjan
Erzerum
Malatya
Diyarbakr
Mosul
Damascus
Medina

Tiflis
Shirwan
Qars
Baku
Tebriz
Ardabil
Sultaniya
Mazanderan
Asterabad
Damghan
Rayy
Qazwin
Semnan
Hamadan
Kirmanshah
Baghdad
Ajami
Dizful
Shustar
Ahwaz
Basra
Isfahan
Yazd
Shiraz
Kirman

Aral Sea
Syr Darya
UZBEKS
Transoxiana
Tashkand
Bukhara
Samarqand
Amu Darya
Merw
Meshhed
Nishapur
Balkh
Khorasan
Herat
Ghur
Kabul
Ghazna
Qandahar

CASPIAN SEA

Azharbayjan
Iraq Ajami
Iraq
PERSIA
Faris
Kirman
The Great Desert
Makran
Sind

Al-Jazira
Syria
Syrian Desert
Arabia
Al-Hasa
PERSIAN GULF

Empire of Shahrukh, 1407–1447
(Ruled by Timurids Till Around 1500)

Other Timurids

Qaraqoyunlu, 1406–1467
with Years of Conquests

Empire of Uzun Hasan Aqqoyunlu
(1467–1477)

Ottoman Territories Around 1490

Mamluks

Dhu'l-Qadar Dynasty

0   100   500   1000 Miles

SAFAWID PERSIA
in the 16th and 17th Centuries

Sinop
Amasia
Batum
Siwas
Kizil
Kayseri
Ersinjan
Erzerum
Trapezunt
Qars
Eriwan
Charpul
Caldiran
Malatiya
Diyarbakr
Urfa
Antiochia
Aleppo
Damascus
Mosul
Baghdad
Kerbela
Najaf
Basra

Georgia
Shirwan
Tiflis
Derbend
Ardabil
Tebriz
Adhar-bayjan
Alamut
Qazwin
Hamadhan
Teheran
Qum
Kashan
Isfahan
Kirmanshah
Luristan
Iraq
Dizful
Shustar
Ahwaz
Shapur
Istakhr
Shiraz
Faris
Kirman
The Great Desert

PERSIA
PERSIAN GULF
Bandar Abbas
Hormuz

CASPIAN SEA

Aral Sea
Syr Darya
Sighnaq
KHANATE OF KHIWA
Urganj
KHIWA
KHANATE OF BUKHARA
Bukhara
Samarqand
Khojanda
Utrar
Soyram
Tashkand
Khokand
Uzkand
Kashgar
SJAGHATAI KHANATE
TIEN SHAN
Issiqkul
Aqsu
L. Balkash

Asterabad
Merw
Meshhed
Damghan
Seuman
Nishapur
Khorasan
Herat
Balkh
Badakhshan
PAMIR
HINDUKUSH
Kashmir
Afghanistan
Kabul
Ghazna
Qandahar
Sijistan
Kirman
Baluchistan
Sind
Kangra
Lahore
Pandjab
Multan
Delhi
Rajputana
Gujarat
Cutch
Cambay
Kathiawar
VINDHYA MTS.
Masqat

ARABIAN SEA

KARAKORUM

Empire of Shah Ismail Around 1512

Eastern Border Around 1506

The Shaybanids

Contested in the Sixteenth Century

Ottoman Sultanate

Territories Conquered by
Ottomans, with Years

Territories Temporarily Held
by Ottomans

Occupied by Ottomans
Reconquered by Persians

Mughul Sultanate of Delhi

Contested Area

Raid of Nadir Shah (1738–1739)

31

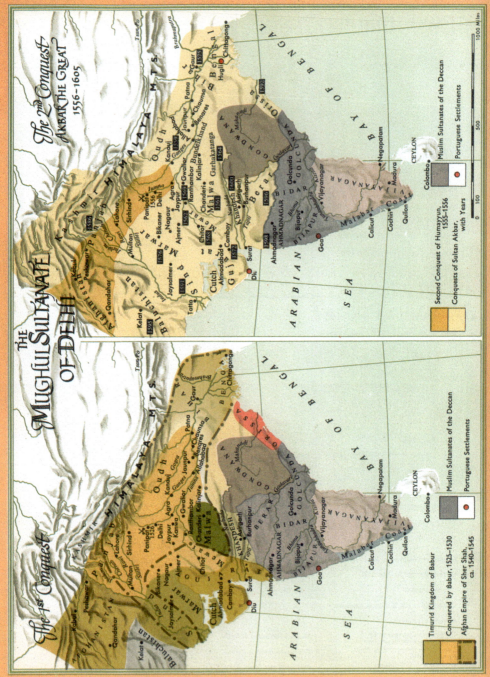

THE
MUGHUL SULTANATE
OF DELHI

The 1st Conquest

Timurid Kingdom of Babur
Conquered by Babur, 1525–1530
Afghan Empire of Sher Shah, ca. 1540–1545

Muslim Sultanates of the Deccan
Portuguese Settlements

The 2nd Conquest
AKBAR THE GREAT
1556–1605

Second Conquest of Humayyun, 1555–1556
Conquests of Sultan Akbar, with Years

Muslim Sultanates of the Deccan
Portuguese Settlements

32

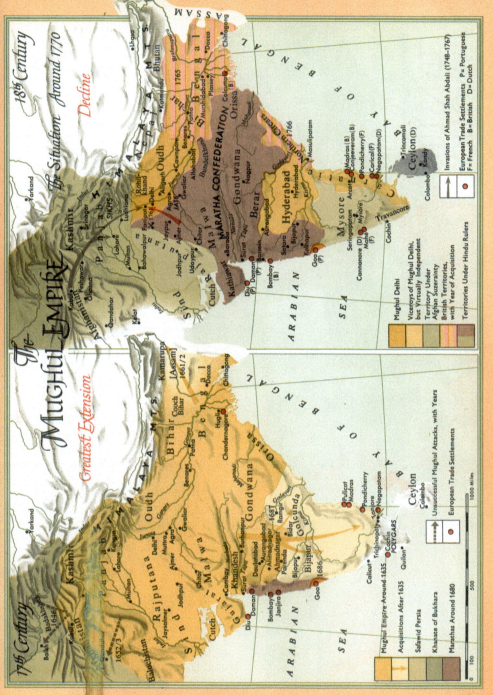

The Mughul Empire

17th Century
Greatest Extension

18th Century
The Situation Around 1770
Decline

Greatest Extension legend:
- Mughul Empire Around 1635
- Acquisitions After 1635
- Safawid Persia
- Khanate of Bukhara
- Marathas Around 1680

Unsuccessful Mughul Attacks, with Years
European Trade Settlements

0 100 500 1000 Miles

Decline legend:
- Mughul Delhi
- Viceroys of Mughul Delhi, but Virtually Independent
- Territory Under Afghan Suzerainty
- British Territories, with Year of Acquisition
- Territories Under Hindu Rulers

Invasions of Ahmad Shah Abdali (1748–1767)
European Trade Settlements
F = French   B = British
P = Portuguese   D = Dutch

Places and regions (17th century map):
Balkh, Badakhshan 1646, Kabul, Kandahar, Kabulistan, Afghanistan, Kashmir, Srinagar, Kangra, Multan, Lahore, Delhi, Muttra, Agra, Gwalior, Ajmer, Joysalmer, Jodhpur, Chitor, Udaipur, Rajputana, Sind, Cutch, Gujrat, Cambay, Surat, Diu Daman, Bombay, Janjira, Calicut, Cochin, Quilon, Malwa, Chanderi, Khandesh, Doulatabad, Ahmadnagar, Aurangabad, Bider, Parenda, Bijapur, Golcunda, Goa 1686, POLYGARS, Trichinopoly, Tanjore, Pullicat, Madras, Pondicherry, Negapatam, Ceylon, Colombo, Benares, Patna, Ganges, Jumna, Allahabad, Oudh, Bihar, Bengal, Orissa, Gondwana, Dacca, Chittagong, Cooch Bihar, Kamarupa [Assam] 1661/2, Hugli, Chandernagore, Godavari, Kistna, Ramgir

HIMALAYA MTS., PANJAB, BAY OF BENGAL, ARABIAN SEA

1652/3

Places and regions (18th century map):
Yarkand, Lhasa, Bhutan, Kathmandu, Kashmir, Srinagar, Peshawar, Ghazni, Afghanistan, Kabul, Kandahar, Kalat, Bahawalpur, Multan, Lahore, Ludhiana, SIKHS, PANJAB, Delhi, Panipat, Jaypur, Agra, Jumna, Aligarh, Cawnpore, Rohilkhand, Oudh, Allahabad, Bundelkhand, Gwalior, Chitor, Udaypur, Jodhpur, Rajputana, Baroda, Surat, Taptu, Cutch, Kathiawar, Diu Daman (P), Bombay (B), Goa (P), Bassein, Kolhapur, Bijapur, Satara, Aurangabad, Nagpur, Hyderabad, Berar, Gondwana, MARATHA CONFEDERATION, Malwa, Bengal 1765, Murshidabad, Plassey, Calcutta, Cuttack, Orissa 1766, Masulipatam, Hyderabad, Mysore, Seringapatam, Mysore (F), Mahé (F), Cannanore (D), Cochin, Travancore, Madras (B), Conjeeveram (B), Arcot, Pondicherry (F), Carical (F), Negapatam (D), Trincomali, Ceylon (D), Kandy, Colombo, Chittagong, Dacca, Kamarup, Monghyr, Patna, Benares

ASSAM, HIMALAYA MTS., Bay of Bengal, ARABIAN SEA, Bengal 1766

33

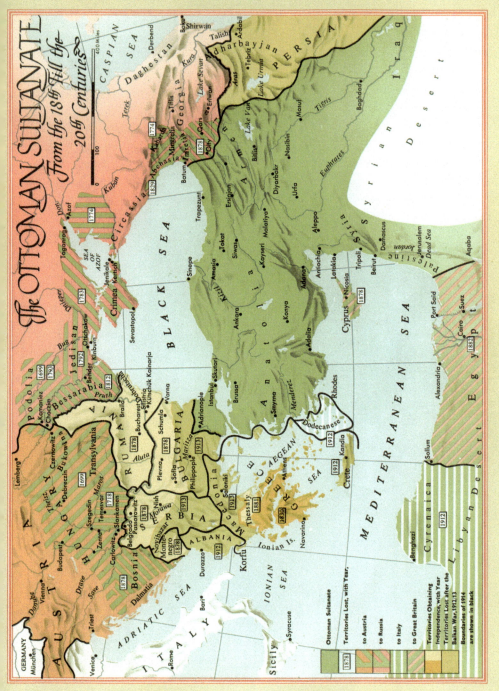

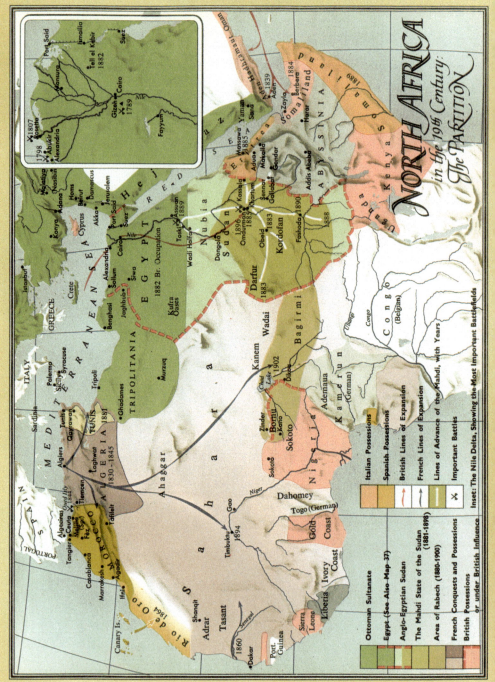

NORTH AFRICA
in the 19th Century:
The PARTITION

Inset: The Nile Delta, Showing the Most Important Battlefields

Legend:
- Ottoman Sultanate
- Egypt (See Also Map 37)
- Anglo-Egyptian Sudan
- The Mahdi State of the Sudan (1881-1898)
- Area of Rabech (1880-1900)
- French Conquests and Possessions
- British Possessions or under British Influence
- Italian Possessions
- Spanish Possessions
- British Lines of Expansion
- French Lines of Expansion
- Lines of Advance of the Mahdi, with Years
- Important Battles

36

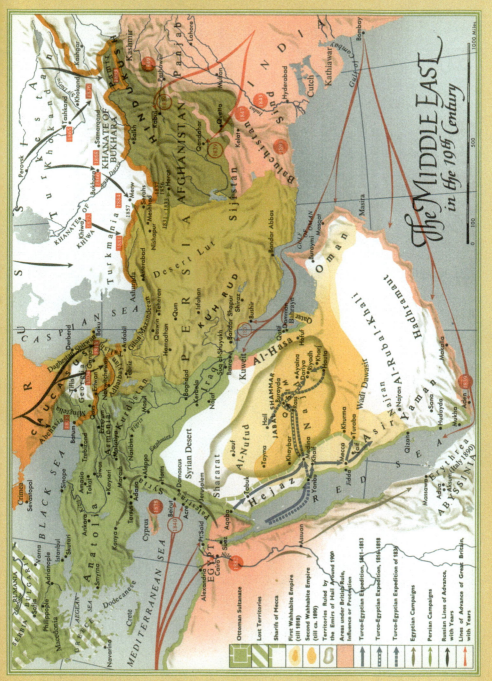

The MIDDLE EAST *in the 19th Century*

0   100   500   1000 Miles

Legend:

- Ottoman Sultanate
- Lost Territories
- Sharifs of Mecca
- First Wahhabite Empire (till 1818)
- Second Wahhabite Empire (till ca. 1890)
- Territories Ruled by the Emirs of Hail Around 1900
- Areas under British Rule, Influence or Protection
- Turco-Egyptian Expedition, 1811–1813
- Turco-Egyptian Expedition, 1816–1818
- Turco-Egyptian Expedition of 1835
- Egyptian Campaigns
- Persian Campaigns
- Russian Lines of Advance, with Years
- Lines of Advance of Great Britain, with Years

RUSSIA

Turkhokandetan · Perovsk · Tashkand · Khokand · Kashgar
Samarqand · KHANATE OF BUKHARA · Bukhara
KHANATE OF KHIVA · Khiva · Merw · Turkmania
Balkh · HINDU KUSH · Kabul · Peshawar · Kashmir · Lahore
AFGHANISTAN · Herat · Qandahar · Quetta · Kelat
Mehhed · Serahs · PANJAB · Multan · INDIA
Nishapur · Asterabad · Sijistan · Baluchistan · Sind · Hyderabad · Kathiawar
Desert Lut · PERSIA · Teheran · Qum · Qazwin · Cutch · Gulf of Cambay · Bombay
CASPIAN SEA · Baku · Derbend · Shirwan · Gilan · Mazindaran · Isfahan · Shiraz · Bondar Abbas
CAUCASUS · Tiflis · Erivan · Tabriz · Bondar Shapur · Bushir · Masira
Daghestan · Georgia · Nakhichevan · Hemedan · Bondar Shapur
Mingrelia · Abchasia · Armenia · Kurdistan · Baghdad · Qetf · Domman · Bahrayn
BLACK SEA · Batum · Erzerum · Mosul · Kerbela · Basora · Bahrayn · Qatar · OMAN · Burraymi · Masqat
Trebizond · Malatya · Nasibin · Najaf · Suq el-Shuyukh · Kuweit · AL-HASA · Hofuf · Khari · Haufa
Sivas · Diarbekir · SYRIA · Tigris · Euphrates · Iraq · Buraydia · JABAL SHAMMAR · Ross · Riyadh
Ankara · Koyseri · Marash · Aleppo · Homs · Damascus · Syrian Desert · Al-Nufud · Hail · Qasim · Khurma
ANATOLIA · Konya · Adana · Tarsus · Palestine · Jerusalem · Shararat · Tayma · Khoybar · Medina · Mecca · Turuba · NAJD
Smyrna · Cyprus · Beirut · Acre · Aqaba · Tabuk · HEJAZ · Yonbu · Taif · Qizan · ASIR · Najran · Al-Rubal-l-Khali · Hadhramaut
ISTANBUL · AEGEAN SEA · Dodecanese · Crete · MEDITERRANEAN SEA · PrSaid · Suez · Jidda · RED SEA · Sana · YEMEN · Mukalla
Navarino · GREECE · Macedonia · Philippople · Adrianople · Sofia · BULGARIA · SERBIA · RUMANIA
Sevastopol · Crimea · Varna · Skutari · Sinope
EGYPT · Alexandria · Cairo · Nile · Assuan · Qizan · Hudoyda · Mukha · Aden · Massawa · Abu · ABYSSINIA · Erythrea (Italy 1890) · Aksum (Italy 1890)

37

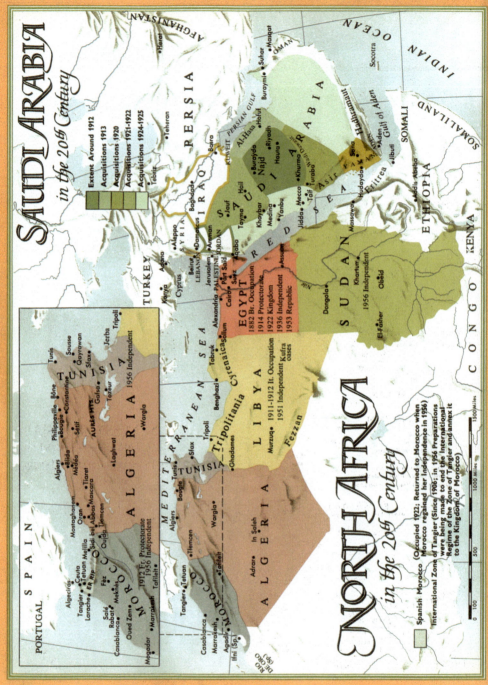

SAUDI ARABIA
in the 20th Century

Extent Around 1912
Acquisitions 1913
Acquisitions 1920
Acquisitions 1921-1922
Acquisitions 1924-1925

NORTH AFRICA
in the 20th Century

EGYPT
1882 Br. Occupation
1914 Protectorate
1922 Kingdom
1936 Independent
1953 Republic

LIBYA
1911-1912 It. Occupation
1951 Independent
Kufra oases

SUDAN
1956 Independent

TUNISIA
1956 Independent

ALGERIA
1956 Independent

MOROCCO
1912 Fr. Protectorate
1956 Independent

Spanish Morocco (Occupied 1922; Returned to Morocco when Morocco regained her independence in 1956)

International Zone of Tangier (Since 1906; in 1956 Preparations were being made to end the International Regime of the Zone of Tangier and annex it to the Kingdom (of Morocco)

0   100   500   1000 Miles   1500 Miles

PORTUGAL

SPAIN

MOROCCO

ALGERIA

TUNISIA

AURES MTS.

MEDITERRANEAN SEA

RIO DE ORO (Sp.)

Ifni (Sp.)

38